Change Your Perception
Change Your Life

Justin Harmon

Change Your Perception, Change Your Reality

Authored by Justin Harmon

Published by The Difference Press, Washington DC
The Difference Press, and the wax seal design are registered
trademarks of Becoming Journey, LLC

ISBN: 978-1-936984-24-4
Library of Congress Control Number: 9781936984268

Art direction by: Ann Alger
Cover design by: John Matthews - bluebullseye.com
Interior design by: John Matthews - bluebullseye.com
Edited by: Sarah Vedolich

Advance praise for Change Your Perception Change Your Life

"True wisdom is the ability to have both clarity and curiosity. This book beautifully marries the collective experience of its guest authors with the genuine curiosity and guidance of Justin Harmon. Reading this book feels like an exploration and a resource; a reminder that living purposefully, doing great work, and enjoying the ride is not only possible, but profoundly practical. A truly inspiring read!"
- **Meg Worden,** *Feed Me Darling*

"A rich life is built by overcoming fear, fostering happiness, and choosing freedom. To do this, you've got to control your expectations and your perceptions. This book is packed with practical tips to help anyone change the way they view the world and start living a richer life today."
- **JD Roth,** *More than Money*

"This book fuels the fire within you to break free from social dogma and live a meaningful life. It connects you to your dreams that had been subdued by the status quo. It is a powerful call to action, to help you become the person you are meant be. A must read for all those aspiring to build their own business, regain freedom, and live fully."
- **Debashish Das**

"I have been struggling with uneven dedication and progress and I didn't know up till now that it happens to others too and it may very well be absolutely normal. It takes a huge amount of stress off of me knowing that it is okay to underperform at times. Change your Perception, Change your Life has shown me how to welcome fear as a sign of something exciting ahead and learn to use it as a tactic for change. This book has some superb advice and tricks that I've yet to try out but will surely be beneficial!"

- Berta Pirchala

"Change Your Perception Change Your Life" by Justin Harmon isn't a book, it is an expedition of the non-conformists soul. He has created a literary symphony of stories and experiences that bring the reader through a fascinating and insightful journey. If you are a soul searcher, or visionary in the making, CYPCYL will help you know that you are on your way to your true self. If you have been down your own path and are creating the life you have dreamed of, CYPCL is like looking into a spiritual mirror and the words will move you."

- Brooklyn Fisher, *YoGirly.com*

"If you're considering reading this book, it's because you want to change your life. Whatever your reasons may be, they exist not because of how your life is (in reality) but because of how you perceive your life to be (YOUR reality). In this book, Justin Harmon and his team will show you how you can reclaim your role as the creator and leader of your life. Above all else, I wish that this book inspires you to take action and make a meaningful impact in the World!"

- Bruno Coelho

"Change Your Perception, Change Your Life will inspire you to see an alternate way living, one where dreams really do come true and the status quo is merely an option you can choose to leave behind. It's full of amazing contributions from some of the biggest thinkers online and will inspire you to think bigger and do more than you ever thought possible. It's full of truth, insight and those rare nuggets of gold that have the potential to swing your thinking and life 180. If you're looking for answers, inspiration or just a push in the right direction Change Your Perception, Change Your Life will get you there."

\- **Michaela Cristallo, *For the Creators***

"This is not just a book; it is a heartfelt message to the world." These are the words in the introduction to the book. Indeed, this is true! This book is not just a book, it can become a life-changer, a mindset shifter, a fear removing shield. Change Your Perception Change Your Life is full of beautiful stories from real people who have made that all-important perception shift of the mind, changed their lives, and in doing so, changed the lives of many others. This is the kind of book you want to hold onto forever, and reread when you need to refuel, and share with your children one day. Inspiring, useful, practical, achievable and enjoyable!

\- **Jesicka Labud, *TwoNonTechies***

Introduction

This is not just a book; it is a heartfelt message to the world.

A message of an alternate way of life – one where you take responsibility for a meaningful future for yourself and your family; one where you can be happy and contribute fully, and not be held back by the prevailing status quo of society.

However, there are some challenges that stand in the way. Change is hard and changing your perception of life, a redefining of all the rules you once knew, is now going to take an incredible amount of effort. It is a difficult road to walk and sometimes your courage fails you. It is the support of the like-minded people in your corner that will carry you through these tough times. My story is similar and my message embodies it as well.

This message about changing perception and transforming lives is enriched by the invaluable contributions from others like me. I want to wish a warm thank you to those who contributed to this book. Your dedication to helping others, following your dreams, and making a positive change in the world are admired and appreciated.

The message that follows is the collective voice of all contributors. I hope it serves as an inspiration and empowers you to find and become the person you were meant to be. The person the world deserves. And the person you have been waiting to become.

Your dreams are yours to take hold of, believe in, and follow. The central message of this book is to see your life and the world in a way which allows you to start a journey towards your dreams and keep moving forward towards them until they are no longer dreams, but your current reality.

Shared here are essays from those who have been on the journey to change their lives by following their dreams, believing in doing what they love, and making a meaningful impact in the lives of others. From some of the top online thinkers and entrepreneurs, to the next generation of difference makers, to those who have just started the path towards fulfillment and purpose, they all share their experiences, insights, ideas, strategies, and speak from the heart on what it takes to truly make everlasting change and take control of your life.

From changing the way we view the world to dealing with the fears and setbacks of the journey towards freedom in our lives, these essays are sure to inspire anyone who wants to follow their dreams, live a life of meaning and purpose, or just want to find more fulfillment and happiness in their lives, to do so with openness, clarity, and a renewed ability to believe it's possible.

Table of Contents

For Roxy,
The day you came into the world was the best day of my life. You're the inspiration that keeps me going. May you grow up to follow your heart, follow your dreams, and create your own path to happiness.

Section One: Change

A Vision for the Future

Sometimes when I look into the future and think about what's in store for my family, me, and the world, I wonder if it will be a future of my own making.

I wonder if at the end of this journey I'm on, I'll be able to look back and say, *"I did the best I could to become the person I've always wanted to be."*

I never thought that was too much to ask of myself, so I decided to take a chance to start something I had no idea how to finish. I saw a vision for the future of how life could be for my family, me, and the world we live in.

I wanted to do something more with my life than just rot away at a blue collar job that I hated, unable to adequately provide for my family. That just isn't me. I wanted to find fulfillment and abundance in my life. I wanted to show others who were in a similar situation what was possible for their lives if they changed their perception and started following their dreams. I ended up finding passion through writing, inspiration through connection with others, and an ever growing desire to change the world.

It's a path of highs, lows, and many choices. If those choices are made with another's interests in mind, you will evolve and progress much faster. I've come to see life as a mirror image of what is already inside of us. We have the ability to create with our perception, thoughts, relationships with others, and connection to the greater awareness--which must be found through belief, faith, and the ability to have an open mind to the truth.

The truth is that your world is my world and that's what we should do whatever we can now, to create a better life for tomorrow.

How to Change the World

Do you ever think about the way you're living your Life? Do you ever just think it's finally time to wake up? To get in touch with the inner part of you who wants to do something different?

Why do we often treat our lives as if there are only certain ways to live them?

I tried to figure this out for years. And for years, I only became more and more frustrated. I didn't agree to go through life just doing what I was "supposed" to do.

Sure, I might be able to work really hard and get a decent paying career. Then, I might actually be able to afford to spend more money on useless crap that someone else said I should buy.

That might be good for some people, but for me and for most of people, money doesn't equal happiness. In fact, most people dislike the work they do. What does that tell you?

It told me that I shouldn't keep going that route. Unfortunately, eight years and 30 some jobs later, I finally just gave up. I gave in and found a good paying job that I disliked, in order to provide for my family. That was fine. It's what needed to be done.

Although I may have done what was necessary at the time, this decision didn't encompass my feelings about what my life's plans were. It didn't contain my passion for wanting to do something different with my time here on Earth.

Through this process of coming together, in a spiritual sense, I found my answers and started doing what I love. I want you to be able to do the same.

I want you to know that it is possible to live your life the way you want. That's what <u>Unplugged Recreated</u> is all about.

You will learn that by unplugging yourself from your current perception of reality, you will be able to create the perception of the world the way you were meant to see it.

I want you to see the world in a way where anything is truly possible because you are the one in control.

The world as we see it today is evolving, simultaneously getting both worse and better.

The world is getting smaller as we connect with every part of it through business, education, and knowledge.

On a global scale, it is not hard to see how everything we do has an effect on something else – either from a political or environmental standpoint, the choices we make echo throughout the globe. **By uniting as one people, one world, and one universe, we begin to follow the law of nature**. As of now, not much of humanity follows the law of nature, simply because we do not see it.

Is it My Ego?

We are wrapped in our egos- our shells which are out for individualistic needs. This shell is beginning to crack and our way of life is changing. There is evidence everywhere of the changes that are occurring in the world.

The information-technology age is turning what once was a big world into a global village. Everyone who lives in the global village should be treated as equals. Yet, social justice evades us and most of us go on with our everyday needs and struggles, without caring what goes on in other parts of the world.

This too, is changing. There have been many protests and demonstrations around the world, some without clear objectives or demands, other than the demand to be treated better. Groups such as the

Occupy Movement in the United States or the tent cities in Europe are all demanding change. A change for the better is in order. When we start to realize the changes that are needed, we see the world for what it is, and understand how we can become an integral part of it.

There are other groups already speaking with the world's experts in science, business, and politics; spreading awareness of mankind's suffering, what the causes are of the blows mankind is suffering from, what we can do to fix it, and the steps needed to address this issue.

New organizations are emerging with a common message for change on a global scale, social justice for all, and an opportunity for everyone to have a fulfilled life without facing suffering, homelessness, starvation, hate, and genocide.

The mass population, one that is awakening to the needs and changes of our world and society, is doing what needs to be done to make the changes possible.

This is a transition period. As we roll with the changes and take action as individuals, we move closer to all of humanity living as one.

Finding Freedom in Discomfort:
A Life-Changing Practice
with Scott Dinsmore

Think back on a time when you were ridiculously uncomfortable. Perhaps even terrified. Your palms are sweaty, your heart's pounding, and it's tough to sleep. I'm talking about a feeling you'd do almost anything to avoid.

Got it? Ok, now what caused it? Whatever created it, chances are you are a better person as a result.

If you ever find yourself stuck in a rut, making zero headway on your big plans, you can bet it's because you're scared. Scared of the uncomfortable.

The biggest killer of progress I've seen with friends, clients and myself, hands down is comfort. To have a chance at living the extraordinary life, we have to get uncomfortable.

As humans we naturally do all we can to avoid pain and seek pleasure. Unfortunately this causes one to settle for mediocrity, leading to a whole host of problems. Not the least of which is fearing your path and living your purpose. You'll simply find too many excuses.

Freedom comes at a price. Earn it.

When was the last time you got something super rewarding, with lasting value, without having to put some serious heavy lifting into making it happen? Other than fluke incidents, the true rewards do not come without taking some risk. You must earn your freedom.

We've come to think all pain is bad (here I refer to pain as discomfort and not the physically harmful and dangerous incidents most of us associate with the word). But the right pain is a crucial part of getting the best out of life. It's what makes goals, accomplishments and victory so desirable. Without the effort, we wouldn't value them. It's responsible for close to 100% of our development. Without pain, you'd surely never reach your potential.

When you're uncomfortable, you're growing.

If you could pick one rule to experience amazing things, I suggest: **If it feels uncomfortable then you're doing something right.**

The only way to experience a dream is through a little healthy discomfort.

Unlike a hiking boot that's too small, this type of discomfort is what makes life rich. To really have a shot at living on your terms, the only choice is to learn to love it.

Life begins just outside of your comfort zone. That's where the magic happens.

- It's the last few brutal reps at the gym that create the results.
- The torture of public speaking makes the best influencers and communicators.
- The terrifying job interview may give you a shot at your dream career.
- Starting a business initially exposes life's darkest doubts but it's the price you pay to do what you love.
- It's intimidating to ask someone on a date but it's the only way you'll find your soul mate.
- Publishing your writing risks a world of criticism but it gives you the chance to be discovered.
- Switching to a healthy diet is brutal at first but is the foundation of an energy-rich, beaming life.

All of my most amazing life experiences have been a result of major initial discomfort: moving out of the country, starting my investment fund, beginning to write and coach, teaching my first speed reading class, proposing to my wife. The best fruit really is out on the furthest limbs.

Don't worry about the fear. It's natural. All the growth comes from stepping into the unknown and trying new things. They will be uncomfortable. You will find a thousand reasons to put it off. You'll think of quitting. But that's what makes the experience that much more amazing. Embrace it. Allow the fruit to ripen. Then begin the feast.

Take the Comfort-Killing Challenge.

The only way to break loose is to go at it head on. Instead of avoiding these uncomfortable situations, commit to doing the opposite. **Do something that makes the hair stand up on the back of your neck.** When opportunities come up, dive on them. You'll know when they do because you'll feel it in your gut. That feeling won't go away unless you confront it. Once you overcome it, your standard of what's possible will rise and the world will be in the palm of your hands. I first learned of the comfort challenge from Tim Ferriss and it's made all the difference.

Agree to get out of your comfort zone at least once a week.

Here are a few ideas:

- Volunteer to give a talk to a group of friends or office mates. Any speech at all will do.
- Start a conversation with someone new. Ideally an attractive member of the opposite sex if you're single. Start with a smile.
- Call a celebrity or famous mentor of yours and ask them 3 questions. Make them meaningful.
- Negotiate a better deal on a fixed price item at a retail store. Don't let them tell you no.
- Pitch an idea to someone who could help make it a reality.

Once you've done a few weeks of the above, switch to daily comfort challenges for a week. You'll be changed for good.

It never goes away.

The only way to avoid discomfort is through inactivity, i.e. laziness. Say no to every opportunity that crosses your path and you will be free of the anxiety that comes with stepping outside your zone. But be warned that with inactivity comes boredom. Your learning and growth will end. Without growth comes death. The first to die will be your passion and love for life. And if it goes on long enough, the rest of you will follow. No kidding. It's these moments of truth that make us come alive.

Even little things can make all the difference. Last week I was invited to a small organic farming event at my favorite olive oil shop. I couldn't find someone to join me, and almost didn't attend for fear of not knowing anyone. Then I sacked up and went anyway, only to come away with my best local S.F. experience yet, and a handful of inspiring friends, including a very cool French wine maker.

Let discomfort ignite your breakthrough.
Most people will stay in a job that makes them want to poke small pins in their eyes for no other reason than it's comfortable. There's no more dangerous place to be. When things are comfortable or manageable, there's no motivation to make a change for the better. Don't let fear of the worst case scenario suck you into this fate. It's never as bad as it

seems and the opportunities will be worth their weight in…well, your freedom.

It takes courage to try new things. It takes courage to blaze your own trail.

The crowd lives in comfort. An extraordinary life thrives in testing the limit.

Scott Dinsmore is the founder of LiveYourLegend, where he writes and helps people discover passion & purpose and do work they love. Check out his latest articles or download his free Epic Work Toolkit.

Waiting for a Glitch
with A.J. Leon

Within 58 seconds after the NASDAQ bell rang on October 4, 2012, Kraft Foods stock price soared by 29 percent. Why? Because of a software bug. For about an hour, a glitch in the system made a few thousand people instantly wealthier with no effort whatsoever. The NASDAQ OMX later canceled all trades before 9:37 in order to mitigate the issue; I read about this in the Economist and found it amusing. And then, a little disconcerting when I thought of all the people I know that are waiting for a glitch. Waiting for a magical hiccup in the system to change the trajectory of their one and only life.

I watched an interview that my friend Jonathan Fields produced with Seth Godin. The most interesting moment, for me, was when Seth was talking about his recent successful Kickstarter project to pre-fund his new book (side note: it was fully funded in like three seconds), and said something to the effect of "this didn't work because I'm Seth." Of course, he's right. It worked because he has spent years, like any true artisan, crafting his work very publicly, and maintaining a platform in which people/advocates/backers/disciples can pay attention to and critique that work.

But Seth's right.

Many people will say, "Sure, he can do that, he's Seth." As if somehow, there's a glitch in the system for smart bald guys who wear awesomely bizarre colored glasses. I mean, he received 900 rejection letters before publishing his second book! A couple months ago, I had someone send me a note that said, "I can't wait to be as successful as you, so I can start changing the world." By changing the world, he was referring to the social projects I have initiated in South Sudan, Kenya, Ethiopia, Tanzania and most recently Malawi. What he doesn't realize, is that in a very non-figurative sense, I emptied my bank account to work on my first social project. I had like 94 followers on Twitter when Melissa and I flew to Africa with exactly one hundred and thirty four dollars in our checking account to help kids in the third world get on the Web, and to raise a few thousand dollars to help change their lives.

Sure, there are glitches.

Maybe you'll win the lottery. Maybe your rich aunt will leave you a Rolls Royce in her will. Maybe your next fundraising campaign with get the attention of my buddy Mr. Brogan and his legions will get behind it. Maybe you'll slip in a Wal-Mart and you can sue them for a million dollars. Maybe a publisher at Penguin will find your latest post and beg you to publish with them. Maybe you'll get re-tweeted by @BarackObama and you'll get 1,000 new subscribers to your blog. Maybe one day all of your stars will line up.

Or. Maybe you'll recognize that the stars are deceiving vixens and that they rarely line up. That risk and courage and rejection and failure are usually key ingredients on a hero's journey. On a path towards doing work that actually matters. Waiting for a glitch is a dangerous gamble.

And it rarely pays off.

AJ nomads around the world and makes things happen. He is a writer, designer, entrepreneur and humanitarian that has initiated social projects in South Sudan, Kenya, Ethiopia, Tanzania, Malawi, The Philippines and England. He is the author of The Life and Times of a Remarkable Misfit *and publishes weekly articles at* Pursuit of Everything.

On Dreams
with Srinivas Rao

Some people decide to follow their dreams. Other people are forced to follow their dreams because they've never been picked. I fall in the second camp.

I've been fired from almost every job I've had.
I've never been promoted at a job.
I kept ending up in the wrong place at the wrong time.

So in some ways, my current path chose me as much as I chose it. But that didn't come without plenty of resistance. I've spent the better part of my life forcing square pegs into round holes, wondering why they wouldn't fit. I was determined to become the poster child for society's life plan. Eventually, I realized that that was never going to happen because I am, in all my glory a complete and utter corporate misfit.

Following dreams isn't about developing super powers. It's about putting one foot in front of the other and taking steps forward even though you don't ultimately know where you're going to end up. It's about the willingness to use a compass instead of a map. It's the scenic route through life: a road filled with potholes, wrong turns, and serendipity. It's about having the guts to keep going long after the average person has quit.

Of course, it's all easier said than done. That's where I believe a spiritual practice comes in. The mind loves to piss in your field of dreams. For me, that's been surfing because it stops the mental chatter. It reconnects me with the belief that anything is possible. When you ride a wave, you get a sense for what it must be like to walk on water. It's a poetic dance of possibility that reconnects you with the crazy, wild-eyed dreamer you know as your inner child.

The decision to persevere is rarely the easy choice. But if you want to live a life that most people don't, you have to be willing to do the things that most people won't. In my case that's been a willingness to live at home despite stigma, judgment, and plenty of raised eyebrows. To me, I view my life as an ecosystem. The more diverse the inputs, the richer my life will be. If you understand how to create a supportive environment the rest will fall into place.

Just be sure to avoid or eliminate the toxic people and the pesticides that might end up in your garden.

Dreams are a sign post. They give you a direction to point your compass. But be willing to waver off the beaten path when it makes sense. Open yourself up to the unexpected opportunities. Say yes to things that you might be tempted to say no to.

The opposite is true as well.

Along the path, there will always be people who will encourage you to abandon your journey and return to a quiet life of conformity. After all, your path is not tried and true. It's not safe. You might die (probably not). But nothing makes you feel as alive as realizing you're going to die someday. Your dreams might be written in pen, but realize that every day is a blank page.

BLOGCASTFM Founder/Host Srinivas Rao has been a 2-Time Speaker at Blogworld Expo and was listed on Problogger's Annual List of 40 Bloggers in 2011. His work has been featured on Problogger, GROW, Search Engine Journal, Smart Passive Income, Twitip, Kikolani, Dumb Little man and many other social media and personal development blogs. Since starting BlogcastFM in February 2010, he's interviewed nearly 400 bloggers, authors, and entrepreneurs.

Following my Dream
with Pace Smith

Once upon a time, I followed my dream.

My dream was to be successful. To have a well-paying, stable job that I enjoyed. To make a bunch of money, invest wisely, and become rich.

I went to college, studied computer science and logic, and got a job in artificial intelligence. I gained the respect of my peers, published a paper, and spoke at a respected AI conference. I made a bunch of money, invested wisely, and was well on my way to becoming rich.

I had done it! I had achieved my goal!

So why did I feel so empty inside?
My dream wasn't really *my* dream at all. It was my parents' dream for me. It was the American dream. But it wasn't *my* dream.

I needed a perspective shift. No, that's not big enough for what I needed. I needed a paradigm shift.

What's the point of life? In particular, what's the point of *my* life?

I just didn't know. But the one thing I did know was that the point was not to live a stable, comfortable, complacent life.

The answer jumped out at me one day when I least expected it. I had presented a workshop on relationships and communication. It was fun! And when the attendees came up and thanked me, my heart felt full. The next day, two attendees told me how my presentation had helped their relationship *that very day*, and my heart was overflowing with love.

That was when I found my true dream.

At first I thought my dream was to help people with relationships and communication. But the heart isn't picky. It just wants to help. My dream grew into helping people find their paths in life. Helping people connect with their hearts. Helping people follow *their* dreams.

But there was a giant monster standing in my way.

It was my old dream of having a well-paying, stable job. Of being financially secure. In order to make the leap to follow my heart, I would have to face that monster. I would have to let go of my old dream to follow my true dream. I would have to face my fear of running out of money if I wanted to do what I loved.

I needed a perspective shift. No, that's not big enough for what I needed. I needed a paradigm shift.

Every time I tried to follow my true dream without shifting my perspective, I walked in circles and ended up right back where I had started.

"But that's too risky; I've got to keep my steady day job!"

"I can just help people in my spare time. That's enough, right?"

"But what if I fail?"

So I asked myself again: What's the point of life? In particular, what's the point of *my* life?

To follow my heart. To help others. To love, to be loved, and to be Love.

And that's all. That's everything. Nothing in there about money or security or stability.

The point of my life is love.

I tried to simply snap my fingers and shift my perspective, but it didn't take. My money fear kept sneaking up and biting me, sending me into panic and preventing me from following my dream.

I needed help. I needed support.

I tried about eighty billion things, and the one that worked best for me is the Sufi practice of Remembrance. It's like meditation, but instead of emptying your mind of thoughts, you fill up your heart with divine love.

This practice gives me the compassion I need to heal my heart. This support gives me the courage I need to shift my perspective. This love gives me the strength I need to follow my dream.

My true dream.

Pace Smith is a starry-eyed queer spiritual nomad who loves to play Dance Dance Revolution. A teacher, writer, and coach, she lives a wild crazy meaningful life and helps others do the same. You can find her at PaceandKyeli.com.

You think you're Free?
with Alden Tan

Following your dreams may sound like a bunch of buzz words put together, especially when it comes to "those" successful guys who have made it and are following their own dreams.

But really, following your dreams isn't that hard and it's the way to freedom. What's freedom? It's doing what you love all the time.

Let me break it down for you, before you think that freedom is just another buzz word.

Yeah. For real. Follow your dream for freedom. You do that by doing what you love. And you do that by finding passion.

Look at passion this way: There are many people and institutions out there all too ready to tell you what is true. Schools want to teach you what to learn and what to do with your life. Your friends and family may be even too nice to tell you what is good for you.

You need to know what is true to you. And you find that truth by simply listening to your experience and holding on to the memories it creates.

Now, how do you know for sure what is true AND feel good at the same time? Passion.
That's why passion is the start and path to freedom.
Go get some. Be free.

Alden Tan keeps it real with personal development at his blog. He pulls it off with style by being in your face and not caring about what others think. Check out his free report Revive Your Life *on how to start living the life you want.*

Be the Boss of Yourself
with JD Roth

For a long time, I was unhappy. I was fat, broke, and miserable. Maybe I was depressed, I'm not sure. Whatever the case, I didn't like my life, and I wanted it to change. I waited and waited but nothing different ever seemed to happen.

Eventually, I hit rock bottom. I wasn't willing to allow myself to sink any lower than I had. Though slowly at first, I made changes to my life.

I started by taking control of my finances. I began to read about saving and investing. As I read, I put what I learned into practice. It didn't happen overnight -- in fact, it took years -- but I paid off my credit cards and put money into savings. Today, I'm debt-free and have a substantial nest egg.

After putting my financial house in order, I decided to take control of my fitness. I began to read about exercise and nutrition. As I read, I put what I learned into practice. Again the changes happened slowly, but they did happen. Within a couple of years, I had lost fifty pounds and put on muscle. More importantly, I'd changed my eating habits and made exercise a part of my daily life.

It's been said that success breeds success. That was certainly true in my case. Each positive change I made helped me to understand that I could make other positive changes. I realized that nobody cares more about my life than I do. If I want to be happy, I need to be in charge of that happiness. I can't wait for anyone (or anything) to bring it to me.

I am responsible for my own well-being.

As children, we're conditioned to think that we need permission to do things. You need permission from your parents to leave the dinner table or to go outside to play. You need permission from your teacher to go to the bathroom.

Even as adults, we often feel we need permission. You need permission from your boss to leave work early. You need permission from your spouse to hang out with your friends instead of cleaning the bathroom.

Like many folks, I grew up with an external locus of control. I thought my fate was largely determined by the people and events around me. This wasn't a conscious belief, but it was always there, underlying everything I felt and did. As a result, I waited for things to happen. I needed permission to take risks or to try new things.

That's no longer the case.

I've spent the past 10 years reclaiming my life. I've shifted to an internal locus of control. I've come to realize that I'm in charge of my own destiny, and that it's my responsibility to live a life I love. This means that I need to:

* **Avoid excuses.**
* **Ask for what I want.**
* **Own my decisions.**
* **React constructively to adversity.**
* **Collect (and take advantage of) opportunities.**
* **Let go of the things that no longer work.**
* **Ignore the opinion of others.**
* **Act -- even when I'm afraid.**

If you're unhappy, nobody else is going to make things better for you. You have to make things better for yourself. Concentrate on the things you can control, and use that control to fix the other things that are broken. This will grant you even more control over your future well-being.

You live in a world of your own creation. You have the power of choice. You create your own certainty. Live your life as you want to live it, and do so without regret. Give yourself permission to do so.

Caveat: It's okay to change jobs or to move to San Diego. It's not okay to steal your neighbor's television or to drive on the wrong side of the highway. Remember the Golden Rule. Do what you want insofar as you're not harming others.

J.D. Roth founded Get Rich Slowly, wrote Your Money: The Missing Manual, *and contributes to the monthly "Your Money" column to Entrepreneur magazine. You can also find him at Time magazine's Moneyland blog and of course jdroth.com, otherwise known as* More than Money.

Section Two: REvolution

The Beginning of the End.
Starting Over.

I caught a glimpse of what my life would have been like if I had chosen to take a different path.

It came in a dream. I was walking between some very tall buildings, wearing a fancy business suit, discussing work related issues with an associate (boring stuff, I know).

Moments later, I was being arrested for some kind of fraud and my name was all over the news. I must have been a high profile businessperson and garnered a lot of attention. <–*Narcissistic much?*

When I awoke from that nightmare, it got me thinking. I pondered my life and how I got to where I was at that moment.

I have never cared much for looking at the past, wondering about the decisions I have made, remembering the good times and bad.

I always thought that if I could just go with the flow, things would work out. They did, more or less.

Reality Setting in

After I realized it wasn't cool being a 21-year-old still living at home, bouncing through dozens of jobs, partying without a care in the world, and not taking responsibility for my own life. I decided to figure things out.

Well, I didn't really figure things out. I did hold down a job long enough to afford a place of my own. I became involved in a long-term relationship. I guess I was growing up.

In truth, what I was really doing, was settling.

At the time I didn't have any other choice. At least, that's what I thought based on years of forced education, intended to prepare me for the "real world."

Truthfully, I contest what is considered by "normal" society, to be the "real world." Just because I didn't want to be a working stiff, didn't mean I wasn't living in reality.

I was still going with the flow, you know? At least now I know why they call it "settling down."

It's easy to end up settling for a downgraded edition of a life that could otherwise be used to find fulfillment, follow your passions and dreams, and do something that matters.

Not that I had a plan at the time – which, of course, was part of the problem.

That's a Big Problem

You know it. I know it. We all do. Settling for the whole get a job we don't like to pay for things we don't need, while simultaneously attempting to live a happy life.

Guess what? It doesn't work that way. Studies show that over 80% of workers DO NOT like what they do for a living. And why should they?

Corporations and profit driven stockholders do everything possible to be more efficient and effective in their operations, which in turn has a negative impact on the people they employ. The same people who also happen to be customers.

My point is this- you don't have to settle in life. Everything you have been told about the importance of going to college to get a well-paying job, then finding a career with promise of climbing the corporate ladder is a bunch of bullshit that no longer applies in today's world. Sure it works for some people, but it's not a formula for everyone.

It's the beginning of the end

Today's generations are piecing things together. They are beginning to understand that the society which big corporations and governments are attempting to run, are not compatible with the rest of the world.

There is a new economy on the rise. One that embodies the idea of a connected world and the benefits of using the power of connection to learn, grow, and do things that matter.

As Seth Godin so eloquently termed, we are moving towards a connection economy. Seth says that in the connection economy, there are two kinds of projects. Projects that exist to create connections and those that do not.

The Internet is the embodiment of connection. The possibilities of connecting with hundreds of thousands of like-minded people are endless. This new economy will be one of connection, cooperation, growth, knowledge, trust, honesty, and change.

A change in the way we live, view, and understand each other and our place in the world as a whole.

A change for the better. To do something with your life that matters. To follow your dreams, passions, and ideas.

To become an artist in your own unique way. To create, innovate, and experience the world in a way that is your own. A world inside of you that longs for the day where you bring your desires to life.

The day when you commit to take action, transforming your life to one of purpose. A day when you become inspired to lead with your heart and not with your mind.

You're the Artist

For far too long, people have been writing the same script. The day has come, when we no longer need to follow the path that has been laid out before us.

Now is the time for unlimited possibilities and connections. A world view where you are the artist and life is your canvas.

You can paint, draw, or write whatever you want. It's your life.

Following the White Rabbit

Déjà vu

Have you ever been in a situation, where at one moment or another, you experienced a form of déjà vu?

I have. This is the story of my journey down the rabbit hole and into the land of make believe. It's a tale (sometimes tall) but always stressing a significant amount of truth and meaning.

I've always felt I was on some sort of path. I never knew quite what it was, other than for some reason or another I'd experience strange patterns of familiarity with certain situations and events. I always called these experiences "déjà vu."

Not all of the time, (but often) I would remember a dream I had had regarding my current situation. When a situation came upon me, I would immediately recall whether I had dreamt about it. It might have been a week or several months between the dream and the real-life experience.

Epiphany

Have you ever had a moment in your life, when out of nowhere, you gain clarity to an answer— an answer you're not even sure you were looking for?

That's what happened to me a little over three years ago. It was an ordinary day; I was taking a shower. Life was merely routine.

I remember that at the time, I was pondering and researching spirituality, metaphysics, and other material pertaining to the meaning of life.

Anyway, I was in the shower, the water pouring down on my head. It felt relaxing and gave me a tingling sensation on my freshly shaved scalp. I was just standing there with my eyes closed, when seemingly out of nowhere, I had an epiphany.

It was unlike anything I had ever experienced. I felt an overwhelming surge of warmth and calmness radiating through my entire body. It was a sense of complete satisfaction and total clarity; I knew that it was the answer I had been unwittingly looking for.

It was an air of complete awareness of the essence of life. It was a familiar feeling. A feeling of consciously understanding something of vital significance. Something necessary to helping humanity rise to the next level of existence.

Ready for it? Here it is.
Everything is connected to everything.
Everything is energy.

Now, you need to understand the personal significance of this revelation. I am someone who questions and analyzes everything. However, at that life-changing moment, I was completely immersed in joy and satisfaction for what I had experienced.

At this realization, I immediately went to Google to confirm my revelation. *<--ridiculous, isn't it.*

I couldn't simply trust my higher consciousness. That would be too simple. Instead, I had to Google it.

Why?

Well, doesn't Google connect us to everything? If I can connect to everything through Google and everything is already connected to everything else, I should definitely be able to find out if all of this connection stuff makes sense.

The truth is, of course, that everything is connected.

Seriously. I researched this topic and as it turns out, scientists have discovered that everything is indeed connected to everything else.

Of course, I cannot prove this realization merely, based on my research, but deep inside, I know it's true. It is a truth that defies words and definitions. When you know, you just know.

Either way, this epiphany allowed my true self to slowly surface opening my eyes to the underlying truths, in our reality.

Suffering & Sorrow

This was the pivotal moment when I began searching for the "white rabbit."

I had no idea what I was looking for. All I knew was that there was a reason I had suddenly awakened to something higher than myself. Something had to be done. I did a lot of research, but came up with very few results.

I searched and searched, but this white rabbit was crafty. I would often feel a sense of knowing, only to be hindered by a dozen locked doors. I was lost in my own world, trying to escape from the despair which my journey had led me through.

I was lost, confused, and fearful I would never find my purpose.

It was a time in my life during which meaningless routine, suffering, and negativity flowed abundantly through my veins.

I had created the world in which I was imprisoned. A world where suffering and sorrow ruled over desire and fulfillment. I had created a life isolated from those closest to me. My search for clarity cost me more than I could have ever known at the time.

Fortunately, I was about to discover something incredible at the precise moment I was prepared to embrace it. After nearly eight months of failing to achieve any satisfaction in my life and inner being, I found what I was looking for.

Discovering the Truth

It was at that moment in my life, when I discovered a greater truth inside myself, and fully understood my purpose on this Earth.

Walking the Line Between Fear and Fulfillment

Growing up, I was always the quiet, shy kid who never raised his hand in class. I was the one who never talked to girls and had trouble making friends due to being shy and nervous.

My entire childhood schooling experience was led by fear. I was scared to talk to anyone and utterly terrified to approach someone from the opposite sex. Yeah, girls made me nervous. Still do.

Over the years, the shyness was replaced with anxiety and frustration. I would get mad at myself for not having the guts to do something outside of my comfort zone. Consequently, my teenage years were a wreck. I harbored a ridiculous amount of social anxiety while trudging my way towards manhood.

Along with the shyness, frustration, and anxiety, I started to get depressed. I blamed myself and obsessed over the things I wish I would have done differently. I placed an intense amount of pressure on myself to just start living and stop being afraid. I buried my feelings and emotions, kept my head down, and avoided uncomfortable situations.

Being depressed, shy, anxious, and afraid, just plain sucks. It's difficult to escape from the power that these words can have in our lives. I wish I could say that I have no regrets in my life, but looking back, I wish I would have had more courage to push through my fears and see them as opportunities for growth.

Of course, I also realize, it took being the person I was, to grow into the person I am. I am awake and nearly free of the power of negative emotions; with the ability to use them to my advantage.

The words and feelings I had always felt, started to take on a different meaning when I finally began to understand them. I knew there were many different types of fear, but I wanted to know why they were so difficult to overcome.

Early 20 Something's

When I was in my early twenties, everything started to change. I slowly started to evolve from the shy nervous kid, into a partially confident and self-aware young man. I found it easier to talk to people, and didn't get nearly as anxious in social situations.

The biggest transformation during that time period, or evolution, was my ability to start discovering the real me. I realized I was an introvert, which explained why I was most comfortable living inside myself. I became fearful of how others perceived me and of how I perceived myself.

I did a lot of soul searching. I wanted to be comfortable with myself; to stop caring what others thought. The problem was, I did care. I wanted people to like me, I wanted to be noticed, and I wanted to have the confidence to talk to women.

There was about two or three years of sex, drugs, and rock and roll, and about 30 or so jobs–all of which gave me brief fulfillment. I had some fun, I'm not gonna lie, but genuine fulfillment came when I started to truly understand my inner world and how to use that world to achieve progress in my life.

Searching for Change

I read dozens of books and hundreds of articles on self-improvement. I found that it was rather simple to change my feelings from fear and anxiety into hope and inspiration. So that's what I did. Anytime I began to get a little nervous about an uncomfortable situation, I would recognize it as such, and seek to conquer and overcome.

I tried anything and everything that entered my mind. For example, I found that it was fairly easy to change my emotions by shifting my focus.

As I started to understand that fear was just an emotion stemming from my nervousness in uncomfortable situations, I worked on recognizing the fears that might arise, before they moved to the forefront of my mind.

Using Fear as Opportunity

Once I began to recognize the situations that led to fear of some kind, I realized something very important; my fears always surfaced when a change of circumstances was on the horizon.

Here's an example: I was asked by a friend, to move 3,000 miles away to the west coast, for the sole benefit of life experience.

My first thoughts were, *"I can't leave my job. What about my family? It's too big of a risk. What will I do? What if the people I meet don't accept me?"*

As these familiar doubts and fears immediately rose to the surface of my mind, I realized something. As with most opportunities in life, we weigh the benefits and the potential pitfalls. In order to overcome my fear, I merely had to outweigh it with any and every potential benefit.

I went with a friend to Monterey, California, for just over two months before returning home to Wisconsin. I chose the opportunity of experiencing something new and potentially life changing, *(which it was)*, over the fear of change and the unknown.

Can you guess what happened? I had an amazing time, gained some awesome memories, and met some amazing people. The memories and experiences from those two months will stay with me for the rest of my life.

All because I chose to look at fear as an opportunity to do something remarkable.

I have a few methods I use to overcome the fear and anxiety.

Recognize Fear as Potential Opportunity

Every time I become nervous or afraid I stop and ponder the reason for my fear. Fear always appears before I do something that could potentially impact my life in some way. When the anxiousness and fear starts to raise my blood pressure, I look at the potential benefits of the situation, based on the past, and turn the fear into inspiration and motivation.

I have grown to embrace the feeling of fear. It is fear that makes me come alive, leads me outside my comfort zone, and allows me to change. Every fearful situation gives me both the ability to progress as a person and the opportunity to make a necessary change in my life.

Use Anxiety as a Weapon

In the past, the social anxiety I felt was quickly turned into nervousness, and ultimately became fear. Now, I use my anxiety as a trigger to bring forward the desire, inspiration, and strength to move forward in a situation. I had plenty of written ammunition to turn to for my inspiration. As I learned to think about these things on a daily basis, it became progressively easier to turn those negative feelings into positive ones.

Remember my Purpose

Through all the years of inner fear, anxiety, and frustration, and the battles I fought in my own mind–I now have a desire to follow my passion. By believing in myself and following my dreams of making a difference in the world, I am able to help others believe in themselves and understand the purpose in their lives.

In retrospect, I realized my purpose when I grasped that my life wasn't just about me. When I understood that I could make a difference in my own life and become happy, awake, fulfilled, and truly free–by helping others and making a difference–I began to receive the best gift of all… **Fulfillment.**

Fulfillment from the path I have taken is beginning to take shape. This is evident through the changes I have made and will continue to make on my journey. The hope and inspiration to keep moving forward on my mission to change the world. All of these components continually shape my inner world as well. This has lead me to the understanding that life is more than overcoming fear, anxiety, and adversity– it's about walking the line that between fear and the constant pursuit of fulfillment. Doing so will allow for the greatest growth and change for your life.

At least it has for me.

Changing your Life like a "Boss"

Are you tired of life beating you up at the very moment you think things are turning around for the better?

I know I am.

It can be hard to change your life...to change your circumstances. When you're up, you're up and when you're down, it's hard as hell to get back up again. Maybe that's why some people don't even try at all. They stay down, dragging their way through life, appreciating what they have, and not expecting much more than that.

It seems to me, at least from my perception of things and the physical environment that encompasses me--people don't expect much out of life.

They have given up!

People have given up on trying to do something more with their life than merely achieving the status quo.

It took me 25 years to meet someone who was actually living their dreams.

Now how sad is that?

Where I'm from, (just like so many other environments) people don't follow their dreams...they just try to get by. They are forever engulfed in the bubble offered by society presents. A bubble filled with negativity, inertia, routine, misinformation, mis-education, narcissism, pessimism, boredom, lack of freedom, suffering, and the mere mundane, etc., etc., etc...

Let's face it. It's way too easy to quit on your dreams.

What's even more messed up, is that most people think of dreams as just that… dreams. Something that sounded good in their head, but at the end of the day, isn't even a possibility. This disconnect between imagination and possibility is the reason that the masses never even attempt to dream. People have lost their ability to dream, before they've even tried.

How do you say to someone, **"Hey, you should follow your dreams",** when they are having a hard enough time, getting through the struggle of their everyday life?

Take this story for example: *There's this girl I know who as a child, dreamt of traveling the world. She wanted to see the Great Wall of China, the infamous city of Paris, the feel of the ocean water running between her feet, and the scenic views of the Redwoods in Northwest America. She had a collection of pictures in a chest, of all the places she wanted to travel to when she grew up.*

Can you guess what happened?

I'd like to tell you she is somewhere out there, nomading around the world, seeing all the places she has collected in her chest.

I'd like to say that she followed her dreams, and lives a life full of adventure, joy, love, and fulfillment. I'd like to say it, but I can't.

Nope, this story ends, like most stories do in today's society, with a dream deferred, or worse – abandoned. After graduating high school and taking a break before deciding whether or not to go to college, the girl met a guy, fell in love, got married, and had three children. It wasn't what she planned but it's what happened. She loved her husband and kids, but she didn't love the facing the daily struggle that billions suffer on a daily basis.

She became another victim of circumstance.
She was poor.

Just like the countless others who live day-to-day, paycheck-to-paycheck, the girl and her husband were trying hard just to provide shelter, food, and some form of life in between. If you asked her why she never visited the Great Wall, she would say, "how? With what money?"

She and her husband have tried to put some form of savings in place, but between the costs of raising a family of five on a single yearly income of $30,000, and the realities of circumstance which life brings--they're lucky if they can afford a vacation once every five years. And that's only for a three-night stay somewhere within driving distance.

Being able to fly to Paris, ha! Yeah right! Not in this lifetime, the girl would say.

Circumstances Can Cloud Your Vision

All she sees is how much money it will cost to visit all the places she has ever wanted to go. She looks at her life, her responsibilities, her options, etc.--but to her, it's not a possibility, because she will never have that kind of financial freedom.

Sadly, that's just the problem, isn't it? ***The status quo, strikes again!***

Yet, the girl's story isn't much different from millions of others, playing the same game, with the same type of circumstances. What saddens me most, is that the girl, (and the millions of others who are victims of the same circumstances) are practically clueless as to how or where to begin changing their life and following their dreams. They think it's too late, but the truth is, it's not – it's never too late to follow your dreams.

Outsmarting Circumstance

I've been talking a lot about circumstance. Allow me to be a little more specific. The circumstances we face in our life, and the choices we make during those circumstances, can either lead us to where most of us want to be;

Happiness, fulfillment, freedom, joy...
Or--
They can lead us to a state of being, which delivers more suffering, negativity, doubt, and fear.

The choices you make in life's circumstances, give you the opportunity to change your life, and alter the perception of your reality, one circumstance at a time.

Letting Go

First things first. Before I get to the part where you stop being a helpless victim and begin to face your circumstances, and change your life like a boss, you have to understand something:

> The circumstances we put ourselves in, (*either willingly or not*) and the choices we make, do not matter as much as how we progress and evolve as a person because of them.

> The real changes happen when we stop searching outside of ourselves for answers and instead, look within.

> You are the co-creator of your perception of reality.

> Letting go of what you think you know about your external world will allow you to have an open mind, and acknowledge the possibility of change.

How to Change your Life like a Boss!

If you're still with me, I'll get to the good stuff. Below are some actionable steps you can take;

Learn, Understand, & Use

It's amazing how life can change both in the blink of an eye and over the duration of many, many years. If you're like me, you're sick and tired of being broke, sick and tired—you desire a positive change. Unfortunately, life doesn't change *for* you, *you* have to change it.

You need to educate yourself on the fact that your life is yours to change; you must be an active participant in those changes. You should understand that you are a slave to your very own mind.

Eckhart Tolle explains it like this;
"You are unconsciously identified with it, so you don't even know that you are its slave. It's almost as if you were possessed without knowing it, and so you take the possessing entity to be yourself. The beginning of freedom is the realization that you are not the possessing entity - the thinker. Knowing this enables you to observe the entity. The moment

you start watching the thinker, a higher level of consciousness becomes activated. You then begin to realize that there is a vast realm of intelligence beyond thought, that thought is only a tiny aspect of that intelligence. You also realize that all the things that truly matter - beauty, love, creativity, joy, inner peace - arise from beyond the mind. You begin to awaken."

Learning how to separate yourself from "the thinker" will help you to understand how to change your life. You then begin to understand and use the knowledge you have gained. Eventually, if you keep moving forward and progressing as a conscious human being, you'll become more equipped to owning those circumstances.

You know something many do not... *in order to change your life, you must first change your thoughts. If you've reached the point of changing your thoughts, you're already a boss.*

Want to Change your Life?
Let Go of your Old One.
with Jennifer Gresham

Imagine setting a goal of seeing the world in its entire splendor. You decide to climb a really tall mountain to get the best view. You know it's going to be an arduous journey, but hey, you only live life once.

But how will you get to the top? There's a tangle of paths before you, and signs pointing every which way, some pointing in opposite directions.

You don't have much to go on, so you choose a path that looks well trekked and offers a gentle slope. You see some people up ahead of you, smile and wave. How exciting to finally be on your way!

The hike isn't always so happy-go-lucky. Sometimes you stumble, and there are times you have your doubts. People on other paths occasionally whiz past or laugh uproariously and give you a wink. You wonder if you should switch paths and join them.

But you stick to the path you're on, because you're loyal and you've already invested so much time and sweat.

And then you reach a plateau.

It's not unpleasant really; it's just a dead end. You try to focus on the warmth of the rock, the pretty lichen growing between the cracks. The view is…nice.

Still, it's not where you wanted to go. It's not what you wanted to experience.

As you look over your shoulder to the paths behind you, so much becomes clear.

You've come a long way indeed. But it's obvious that a little more scouting at the base would have helped immensely. You didn't have to go far to see that many of the paths combine, and more than a few lead right off the edge of a cliff.

The peak is still somewhere above you, beyond a layer of fog. There's no guarantee that any of the other paths will take you there. There's not even a guarantee of a better view if you arrive.

You have a choice.

You can either accept where you are as good enough or you can walk back down the mountain, pick another trail based on the new information you have, and aim for the summit.

To go higher, try lighter

The trick is to refuse to allow your past decisions to influence the one in front of you.

Seth Godin, a master of psychology and marketing, recently wrote about the distractions that prevent people from following through on the things they want:

> *People are in pain. Often of their own making, they tell themselves a story that obsesses/distracts and compels them. "I'll never get a movie gig again," "I can't believe they didn't like what I offered," [...]*

If we return to our mountain climbing analogy, it's akin to berating yourself for choosing the wrong path, degrading your confidence in your own navigation, while still being unsatisfied with your current location.

If you decide you're truly happy with the plateau, then sit back and enjoy it. However, if you still want more, keep in mind that being wrong about your destination can sometimes be a happy accident.

But if you're still yearning for what could be, then you have to be willing to let go of where you've been and how you got there.

All that hiking means you'll be faster and surer on your feet. Now you have a map of the alternate routes, so you can make more informed decisions than you did before. You might even convince someone to go along with you, providing companionship and fresh ideas.

Too many people get caught up in their past failures, whether it's changing careers, losing weight, writing a book, or getting out of debt. Without realizing it, they pace the same path over and over again, promising to themselves "this time things will be different," and then are disappointed to circle back to the same, familiar plateau.

There's nothing wrong with looking over your shoulder now and then.   In fact, in the Harvard Business Review, Art Markman suggests we view the past best when we gaze back from the future.

Instead, base your [decisions] (at least in part) on what you hope to say when you look back on your life. You may not always succeed, but are unlikely to look back with regret on those decisions that gave you the opportunity to reach your aspirations. And statistically you are much more likely to look back with regret on the roads not taken.

The toughest challenge most face is lightening their pack.

Learn from your mistakes? Absolutely. But don't dwell on them.

Toss out your assumptions about what you are or aren't capable of. Lose the weight of others' expectations. Untie yourself from the emotion of past events.

When you do that, you just might be surprised to discover what you've been carrying with you all along: a rope for scaling to new heights, a hang-glider that introduces you to challenges and vistas you couldn't have imagined previously.

And if you do that, you won't just be thankful for the crazy, winding journey you've taken to achieve your goals. You'll be proud.
After all, how else will you discover what has been hiding, unused, in your pack?

Jennifer helps people escape unfulfilling careers and discover the work that makes them come alive. She is the founder of the online course, No Regrets Career Academy, and author of the popular career blog, Everyday Bright.

Finding Strength in the Darkness
with Karen Renee

"Don't be satisfied with stories, how things have gone with others. Unfold your own myth."
- *Rumi*

All the inspiration in the world can't change your life, or so you might think as you read the words of men and women who have successfully changed their perceptions of what is possible and are now living incredible stories. When depression is your reality, sometimes all your heart can say is, "If only I weren't depressed, I could find and follow my dreams, too."

But, guess what? Depression can be useful, positive, and motivating. It is one of the greatest tools for growth and wisdom in life.

That sounds wrong, doesn't it? But we're focusing on shifts in perception here, so let's explore this concept and see what happens. Depression is useful in the same way that physical pain is useful. You've heard the horror stories of those who can no longer feel pain. They repeatedly injure themselves and don't notice the wounds, which results in the loss of extremities and even limbs. We need pain to alert us to the need for self-care. We need depression and the associated emotional turmoil for the same reason. It isn't healthy to be an emotional parasite. With the knowledge that something isn't quite right, the investigation for the source and solution can begin.

Sometimes the reason is as obvious as the bone jutting from a broken leg. Death. Bullying. Abandonment. But there are subtler reasons as well. Living in opposition to your core values. Daily effort without a deeper purpose. A lack of meaningful connection in relationships. Having no "why" for your life choices aside from compliance with social, family, or religious legalism and demands, which inevitably results in a starvation of the soul? Personal purpose, meaning, belief, and connection are the nutrients for a stable emotional life, and these cannot be borrowed from others, though you can learn from them. You are constantly constructing your own purpose. And this is where depression's positive effects come into play. Your entire nature will scream with confusion and regret when you attempt to live on someone else's foundation.

You will also feel a sense of relief when your actions align with your own beliefs and values, even when the choice comes with painful social backlash. This is the only place you can start. Eventually, all that is breakable will break. If you accept this fact and free yourself to grow and change, you will eventually discover the strong and unbreakable elements of your existence.

What you have to offer the world is this story of discovery. This is what you find inspiring in the lives of others, and it is what others find to be inspiring in you. They do not need your perfection; they need your progress so they can learn from it as they discover their own meaning and purpose for life. There are many who will find the value in your story. Depression, like pain, is a source of motivation. It cries out, "Something is wrong! Fix it!"

Sometimes the process of discovery or healing will move more quickly with professional assistance. Medications can muffle the feeling so you can explore with less distraction, though they are not a permanent solution unless your only problem is a physical dysfunction.

You can consciously gather the tools needed to study the causes for your depression by choosing to try on new ideas; trying on clothing in front of the mirror of your depression. It is important, however, to dispose of that which doesn't suit you. You will discard so many unsuitable items into the growing pile of the past. But then, there are the garments that are meant for you, the ones that light up your face with purpose and meaning. Those you keep for life, and they are the reason for living. Nobody can change your perspective. They can only shine a light on the possibilities and say, "I think you haven't considered this point," or "Have you tried this?" This is one of the key benefits of reading this book. Yet, with help or without, it is you who will bear the weight and the relief of the process of discovery and growth. It is you who mines the purpose from your experiences.

Learn as you go.
It's useful, true, to have a goal and to feel positive energy flowing through your system, pushing you toward accomplishment. But you don't need to feel or see that motivation in order to move forward. Your current goal may be to discover the source of your motivation so you can tap into it. Choose to accept failure and the shattered path as indicators of growth.

Healing isn't always pleasant. (For physical pain there is surgery, physical therapy, and years of tests and medical trials.) But there is a reason for the process, and there is a stronger healing effect for the internal testing of values than can be found among tangible blood tests and scans, since you will definitely learn something useful from every experience, so long as you're looking to see it. Map your depression, its depths, edges, and insights. When you find a light source, refine your impressions and move forward. You are always creating a path, even when you, yourself, cannot see it. As long as you are moving forward, there is the possibility of a beautiful and inspiring life in the midst of the worst circumstances.

And if you feel you must give up hope ... then give up hope, but keep exploring the lack of hope and pushing those limits. It is by testing the limitations of your understanding that your perspective will be altered. As long as you keep learning, your life will be changed by every experience. Depression isn't a subtraction from your life. It's a mark of authentic experience. And you will exponentially increase its value by accepting its lessons. You can pull positive meaning out of a wasteland of regret by learning from the negative experiences. Good shines brighter against the darkness. Collect those jewels of beauty, relationship, and insight. Eliminate the paths you will not explore again, or at least the methods that aren't beneficial. Releasing them will free your heart for new possibilities.

And you have much more to offer the world having faced depression. Those who use their suffering, failures, and losses for the purpose of growth and discovery are generally considered to be the most inspiring people on the planet, even when they don't live up to their own expectations. The quotes I've included are just a small glimpse of the truth in that thought.

There are at least three essential values that can flow into and through your life, no matter what your circumstances.

1. You can find truth and meaning in the midst of great darkness.

2. You can learn from any experience or person, even when they are entirely wrong.

3. You can love others even when you are not being loved.

If you choose to explore life in search of these treasures and cling to them wherever they are found, then I wholeheartedly believe that you will find yourself overflowing with all the meaning, motivation, and reasons that you need to accomplish a successful journey through time.

Depressed or not, these gifts will give you the strength to change your life.

Karen Renee writes and creates art to transform the average perspective on depression by erasing the common stigma. You are invited to visit Kareneeart.com to join in bringing healing to a shattered world, one beautiful heart at a time.

Section Three:
The Awakening

Planting Seeds of Change through Self Education
with Jesicka Labud

It all started with a small business library, and one book. One book became two, then three, four, ten, fifteen, twenty-five, one hundred…

It was the fall of 2009, and I was sitting in my cubicle of a huge architectural firm, working – with my headphones on – listening to an audiobook. As I sat there listening, I knew I was listening to the words that would plant within me the first real seeds of change. I knew something important was happening to me that day: I once again believed in the possibility of achieving greatness again. I had believed it once before, but I had lost it through many years of working in the corporate world.

It happened again on the subway ride home to Brooklyn. I sat, listening anxiously, waiting for the next morsel of truth to be whispered into my ear. My headphones were on, and I looked around me at all the other commuters- tired, finished for the day- relieved to get away from their bosses, excited for dinner perhaps, to see their kids, to talk to their partners, and most of all, resigned to their reality.

Meanwhile, my ears were hearing the truth about human ability that nobody dares talk about, the curse of dogma and following the masses, and the very real possibilities of dreams achieved, and goals met. I listened fervently to the stories of entrepreneurs- past and present, day and night, how they rose from pennies to building railroads across the United States, putting the first personal computers into our homes, creating movements and revolutions… and no longer was I saying "Who are these people and where do they come from? How did they achieve these great things?"

No. This time I was saying to myself: "Wow. These people were just like me. They came from the same place as me, they had an idea, a burning desire – and unlike most people – they persevered."

I was finally able to connect myself to greatness.

I had a burning desire all along- I just didn't know what to do about it. And of course, that's why you're reading this book. You have a burning desire for change. You just don't know how do start. Well, let me tell you something: you've already begun.

Let's backtrack about 15 years though:

Ever since I was a young student – I can't remember how far back – I was fascinated with stories of great achievers. I devoured books about Martin Luther King, Thomas Edison, and Gandhi. My mom would buy me biographies for kids with pictures. I would read them all- Helen Keller's story, the founding fathers, the great industrialists- but I would never understand how this was in any way connected to me. These books however, planted the first seed in me. The seed of desiring greatness.

Later on, when I realized what I wanted to do with my life (which was to become an architect), it was such a strong desire that I worked extremely hard to get into my dream college. I developed strong ideas of my own, personal moral codes of creation, and read many books on the philosophy of architecture. I also studied under world famous architects. I truly believed that I would be fulfilling my goal of achieving greatness. I thought that after graduation, I would be able to (somehow) build the visions that were in my heart. I had vague plans to work my way up the ladder, to "one day" have my own architectural practice that would build for people who really needed architecture in their village or city.

The reality of the profession hit me hard. I could not believe how different it could be- that all moral codes were thrown away- and design was purely an afterthought. I saw how the architecture workforce was mainly fear-driven. I saw how the profession cannibalized itself by overworking their own people unfairly, underpaying them grossly, and serving only the interests of those with money. I also knew that it wasn't their fault- it was because of dogma and the lack of continued education.

Education. And now we come back to books.

In the middle of all these depressing realizations, I found a very special library. This is where I found the books that I was listening to on the subway ride home (audiobooks and physical books), reading on my weekends, and studying during my lunch hour every day.

In the summer of 2009, I started a job with a huge architectural city agency in downtown Manhattan. My parents were so proud of me. It was a job that was very difficult to get, very stable, and for most people- the end of the road to retirement. My dad literally said to me: "Wow, now you're all set for life." To which I had no answer.

I worked hard to get the job because I knew that in the architecture field, this was one of those rare gems of a job where you actually had a real lunch hour, you got paid decently, and you would get off work at a predictable, reasonable time. (In previous jobs, I was regularly coming home at 10, 11pm every night.) I thought- if I could somehow find a way to have a life besides work, I might be happy. I had friends at this job- people I went to school with. I started the job and for a brief moment in time, thought I was happy. I was optimistic about the future again, and I wasn't so stressed out. And then, just when I thought I was finding peace, I found The Business Library.

One day while talking to some co-workers someone mentioned that there was a library somewhere in our massive office building but that "no one ever goes there." I became very curious about it, and I took that was my cue. I asked around and nobody knew exactly where it was or what I was talking about. Our building had more than 25 floors and three separated elevator banks.

During my lunch hour one day, I took the elevators to every floor to look for it. Finally, when I got out of the elevator bank of the 15th floor, I spotted it, tucked away on the far end of the hallway. I could see into the library because it had a large glass window on one side, with a glass encased door.

When I walked in I noticed that it was about the size of one very large bedroom, shelves lining all the walls, windows on one side, and some tables and chairs facing a ceiling mounted TV, and a few island shelves in the middle. The T.V. was running some financial news. A clerk sat right by the door, which was apparently where you checked books out. He said to me "You're free to check anything out if you work in this building. Just give me your ID and I'll create a new account for you."   I handed him my ID.

I walked around and saw that the shelves were full of all the business books I could ever imagine: How to Run a Business, The Stock Market Essential Guide, Marketing 101, Presentations for CEOs... I also saw a great number of what many people like to call "self-help" books. There were books about Leadership, Courage, Positive Affirmations, and How to Accumulate Wealth... and nobody was in there besides the clerk and me.

That day I took out two books and two audiobooks: *Rich Dad Poor Dad* by Robert T. Kiyosaki, *How to Win Friends and Influence People* by Dale Carnegie, *Think and Grow Rich* by Napoleon Hill, and *7 Habits of Highly Effective People* by Stephen Covey. Walking out with those four books under my arm, I hardly realized that this was a turning point in my life, and that books can have such power over us.

This is how I began my personal journey of self-education. I finished those books within a week and came back for more. The clerk created a limit on how many books a person can borrow at one time because of me. It was 15. I took out 15 books every week. I read, listened and learned. I read these books on the weekends, and listened on my headphones while working, on the subway, and during my lunch hours. I read and read until there were no more books left to read in the shelves of that library. I had exhausted and grown out of that library.

My mind was blown open. I learned about money and how the stock market worked. I learned about businessmen who started out with pennies. I learned how Charles Schwab talked his way into creating the biggest steel conglomerate of all time. I learned how a lowly priest founded the Illinois Institute of Technology by giving the best sermon of his life. I learned how to create amazing presentations for venture capitalists through Guy Kawasaki. I learned about how Jack Canfield sent his manuscript out to hundreds of publishers and got repeatedly rejected before making his millions. I learned how Chrysler built his company with no prior car expertise- by investing his life savings in a car, and taking it apart and putting it back together several times until he understood it. I read about the life of Steve Jobs, and how his vision was made real only through faith in himself when nobody else understood or believed it was possible.

I was re-learning everything that I had read about when I was young and idealistic. I was un-learning what I had been told while trying to climb the slow corporate ladder, un-learning the elitism that keeps people from reading those "self-help books." I was rekindling my own fire, and hearing about the people who truly changed the world in many different ways, and like me, started from essentially nothing.

That meant one thing: I could do it too.

This shift in my mindset only came after I began to educate myself. I took the time to read these books and found all the little steps that others had taken in order to make bigger changes in the future. It all started with this shift in mindset from "maybe one day it's possible" to "this will definitely happen for me if I start now, with these tiny steps."

Educating yourself is the key to shifting your mindset, because what you will find when you read the right books and watch the right lectures- is that it always starts with a burning desire, and then a plan that you follow relentlessly- a plan that is filled with small, possible steps that you can take from day one. By investing the time and the money in educating yourself, you are already taking the first steps toward change.

I was lucky enough to find a whole library of free books, but I don't believe in coincidences- my heart had always been searching for these books and the information within them. When the possibility of educating myself was presented to me, I took action. You have to be ready to take action when the opportunities present themselves to you.

One thing you should know about that business library is this: it was there for every single person in that office building. Many of them were unhappy with their jobs and current situation, and some of them even complained to me about how they wanted change. Most of them are still there! Whenever I told them about the library- and how they should read

Unplugged from the Machine: Recreated to Revolutionize

I've always had a vivid imagination. Whenever I use my creative side, I can imagine something that in my mind, feels more like recalling a memory.

I'm not saying that I think it's real–only that the details can get very specific. Not sure whether this is normal, but it allows me to have a clear image of what I'm thinking.

It all makes sense in my mind. Unfortunately, when I attempt to articulate the words in a normal conversation it doesn't work very well.

It's hard enough writing articles/posts, let alone actually talking through something in a way that makes sense to the person listening. It's a work-in-progress.

It takes me days to write an article sometimes. On the flip side of that, I sometimes write something in a half an hour and ship it, just because.

For now, it's all about progression in my mind, thoughts, and emotions; until I reach a point at which I don't sound like a complete idiot. At the very least, I want to express my thoughts in a way that's easily understood.

You Will Obey

When I was a young adult, I saw a side of life that many people ignore. I saw society for what it is–*A Sham*. Maybe it was my inability to accept the "reality" that I should go to college and get a career–and yet, that's exactly what I ended up doing.

Maybe it was something else, but I started to realize that the giant cogwheel, the machine known as Society–was broken. The ideas, plans, and vision that I had in my mind, were not a part of society's plan for me.

At this realization, I felt broken. I felt like an outlaw, running from my predetermined future. My nonconformist nature was unacceptable for the people in my environment.

If I said I had plans to live life the way I wanted, they would say, *"You are just a dreamer."* If I said I was going to make a difference in the world, they would say, *"There is nothing you can do."*

I was expected to get a job, make a decent living, and maintain the status quo. I was supposed to conform, obey, and keep my opinions to myself.

This was how I saw the world around me. It was a flawed view, which led me to resistance without victory. I didn't want to follow society's rules, but I felt compelled to do so.

This went on for years

After I "settled down," got a job (and stayed there), got married, and had a daughter, I found a new charge for reclaiming my life. That's when I did what any 28-year-old entrepreneurial-minded person would do, I started writing.

I had always wanted to write, but I never actually got around to doing it.

I turned to the Internet and started exploring. I explored and researched how to escape the corporate nightmare to which I was accustomed.

I decided that regardless of the start-up costs, I would find a way to be my own boss, follow my own beliefs, morals, and values, and finally help people change their lives and make a difference in the world.

I was tired of having ideas and dreams but never following through. I finally decided to take action.

I learned everything I could about blogging, marketing, and running an online business. I researched everyone and everything I found, related to online business.

I gained knowledge, experience, and a new found inner need to change the world. I found a community of people who were doing the things I had always wanted to do. They were changing lives and making a difference in the world.

I became a part of that environment. I followed anyone whose beliefs aligned with mine. I created connections with like-minded people. I was proud of what they were doing and I wanted to be a part of it. ***They were a part of a revolution, and so was I.***

Following my Dream

About a year and a half after I began my journey of self-discovery, I decided it was time to share my message of helping people become happy, awake, fulfilled, and free–simply by discovering their inner purpose, following their dreams, and making a difference in the world.

Sharing my message evolved into the website which I run today. The name "Unplugged Recreated" came to me while I was trying to get to sleep one night. I was thinking about a name for my site that aligned with my message.

Unplugged means you unplug yourself from the machine of society. Recreated means you recreate a life for yourself that has purpose, meaning, makes a difference, and allows you to live a comfortable life of financial freedom.

Although I am not yet financially free, I have unplugged myself from the limiting beliefs and imaginary restrictions presented by society.

I have laid a foundation and set a direction for my path to freedom, happiness, and fulfillment. I am supporting and receiving assistance from others who are on the same journey. I've come this far in only eight months. Just think of where Unplugged Recreated will be a year from now.

Assuming I do complete the actions I need to achieve each day, I should make it to where I want to go.

Armed with the proper knowledge and tools, a result of years of researching and learning–will help me on the rest of my journey. A journey is exactly what it is– it's a process. Just like anything else worth doing, it takes time.

Many people in today's world have a problem with doing anything that requires time and effort. We live in an "I want it now" society. That's just not the way it works.

It's time to slow down, discover what really makes you tick, change your life, and change the lives of others. It is time to make a difference. Alone, we can do little– together, we can change the world.

If any of this resonates with your life, perhaps it's time to make some changes. Maybe you should become unplugged and recreated.

Find Your Path

If you want to take action on your journey, change the status quo, and become involved in something that will change your life and the lives of others, now is the time to begin.

There are many roads you can travel on your journey. I can't guide you through all of them, but I can show you how to follow the road that both myself, and many others are traveling.

It's a road that many of us have started to follow and become forever changed–loving what we do, helping others with our messages, quitting our jobs to live on our own terms, and finally becoming truly awake, happy, fulfilled, and free.

Summary of My Path

The road we walk has different names, leads to different places, but ultimately ends with a similar destination. My path includes helping people become awake, happy, fulfilled, and free—helping them to follow their dreams, pursue their passions, get out of their own way, and create their own dream design. I do this by having a website, writing about what I love based on my knowledge and experience, making connections and becoming friends with other people in my niche, and constantly reading and researching something new. I inspire, I teach, I guide, I write, I coach, I learn....I'm an expert.

My journey has taken me to places within myself in which I have discovered my dreams, found the vision for my life, and started working toward achieving my dreams.

The framework is set, the strategies are in place, and it's time to take action.

Blazing your own path on the road to life's most beautiful treasure...true freedom and fulfillment.

Get your FREE **Dream Design** Toolkit at www.ChangeYourPerceptionBook.com

Changing the Status Quo
with Liz Seda

I heard the door of the bathroom creek open and I put my fist in my mouth to stifle the noise. I peeked through the crack of the stall.

Two young women were walking into the bathroom laughing and talking about something. I don't know what because I couldn't hear anything through the roaring of my ears.

They left the bathroom without finding me, and so I continued to sob.

That's how I spent my lunch hour nearly every day of the last three months at my first corporate job. That's how I lost an organ. That's how I finally figured out that my life was far too valuable to be spent crying in a bathroom.

When your job has stressed you out so much that you end up losing an organ, *you realize that there is something seriously wrong with the world in which we live.*

The stress that came from the job wasn't about the workload or the difficulty (although both were very high).

The stress came from oppression and the pressure to conform, and I just couldn't do it.

People would warn me that I wouldn't make it if I didn't conform to company's expectations, but it didn't matter.

I tried so hard. I tried playing the politics game. I tried sucking up and making pretty pictures for management.

I just didn't have it in me.

It didn't take long for me to realize that I don't like anyone bossing me around; including the person that is determining my raises, promotions, and future within the company.

I don't give a shit who you are. If you are asking me to believe in something I don't buy into, I just won't listen to you.

At first I thought that I was a crazy, self-sabotaging psychopath who wanted to live a life of fear and uncertainty until I died of a nervous breakdown.

I wasn't any of those things. I was a free spirited, uncontrollable force of nature that demanded a life on my own terms.

I was so anxious and afraid that I was going to fail at life until I found out that you can't fail at a life you don't believe in.

Failing at life means failing at what you have defined to be the purpose of your life, not what others have defined to be the purpose of everyone else's life.

This was huge for me. This meant that instead of failing at life, **I was an impostor in someone else's life!**

It took me two corporate jobs to figure this out.

It wasn't that the Fortune 500 Company was just too big and oppressive. The last company I worked for was small and gave me a ton of freedom but the same thing happened.

I couldn't live the life of an impostor, so I quit for good.

I promised myself I would never let anyone lure me back into the false sense of security that working for someone else gives you. I'm not cut out for it and I never will be.

Now that I've come to terms with that, I am no longer anxious or worried or afraid of failing. I feel liberated and happy and free and finally in my element. I'm living my life on my terms and I can't fail at that.

I wish I would have known that back then

In the end, I was so stressed out from all of the negative political feedback I received that I endured stomach pains daily to the point where I couldn't even sleep. Not only did I experience emotional pain from the loneliness and the crushing weight of failure to conform and gain acceptance, but I was also in constant physical pain.

I decided to just give up. I hated it and I was glad to let it go.

So then I did what any normal person does. I put in my two weeks and immediately scheduled all of the doctor's appointments I could before losing my insurance.

One of these doctors' appointments led to a shocking discovery: a huge cyst on my ovary that might be cancerous.

They said that because of my age at the time (23), the cyst was undoubtedly stress-induced.

It wasn't cancer, but they did have to remove half of my reproductive system. It was at that pivotal moment when I finally asked myself if any job was worth one of my organs.

Chances are, I would have replied no, no matter what job I had at the time.

I will never let anyone put me under that amount of stress again. I refuse to attempt to live according to someone else's terms when it endangers my health. It's not worth it.

That's how bad it can get if you are a free spirit but refuse to live true to yourself

I promised myself from that day forward, that I would live my life *my way*. Living my life someone else's way nearly ruined me.

Why We Allow the Torture Racks to Break Us

We were taught that good kids respect and listen to their elders, behave, follow the rules, don't talk back to others, etc.

We were taught that complying with other's expectations is *right*, while disobeying their expectations is *wrong*.

We were not given a reason for this expectation. Why was this unrealistic expectation placed on us in the first place? And why, other than that it was coming from an elder, was this expectation 'right?'

The reasoning behind the expectation didn't matter to our parents, or their parents, or their parents' parents.

We were taught to conform.

We were only loved and accepted when we were obedient

We have been socialized to conform, like dogs, from day one.

We go to school and follow the rules, learn the steps, memorize the technique, etc. We have not been taught to think for ourselves, only to receive processes and follow directions.

We were sent to detention for being self-assertive. We were rewarded for being quiet, invisible, not causing trouble.

We behave, we adapt, we become socialized, or 'given over to public ownership' as it's defined in the dictionary.

Our minds weren't nourished and cultivated like they should have been during school. They were manipulated and modified to mold us into a good citizen.

Like a manufacturing line, we all go through this process until we believe that the 'self' is somehow evil, alienating, and hurtful to others.

We have been brainwashed to believe that the only reason to exist is for others; therefore we don't have the right to our own judgments, our own thoughts, and our own paths in life.

After learning by intimidation rather than respect, we have become fearful of expressing our own values, opinions and desires.

We've been conditioned to be afraid of our own beliefs. As a result, we don't dare to think for ourselves or act on our desires.

How to Break Free Instead of Break Down
Start Increasing Awareness

This is a lifelong journey and there's no quick fix, so you've got to be ready to battle it out with me, okay?

Become more aware of your desire to suppress yourself rather than assert yourself.

You don't have to begin asserting yourself right away, although that isn't a bad idea.

But I suggest waiting if you're particularly timid. You may not actually know how to calmly assert yourself.

Take note of when you suppress yourself and think about why you do so.

You'll begin to see patterns.

For example, I noticed that I would always suppress my opinions and fail to exercise Intellectual Independence around 'authority' figures.
Based on that knowledge, I deduced that I held some sort of belief about authority figures that made me afraid to speak my mind.

After much reflection, I discovered my belief that those in authority don't like people who disagree with them. I also believed that it was important to make a good impression in front of authority figures.

I couldn't find a logical reason for this belief, so I began voicing my opinion and asserting myself in front of authority figures.

I never got fired, I never got in trouble, and, all-in-all, I discovered that if someone became angry when I disagreed with them, they had no business holding a position of authority.

More importantly, I let go of the belief that impressing and gaining the approval of authority figures is important.

By dismissing this false belief, I grew less anxious about voicing my opinions amongst authorities.

Question Your Assertions

This statement may seem contradictory to what I've already said, but it's actually completely different. This is about identifying *why* you believe certain things. Maybe there are situations in which you are not afraid to voice your opinion. Maybe you're the kind of person who just says everything on your mind.

Whatever the case, I want you to pick one aspect of your life and begin to question your beliefs on that topic.

Maybe it's your beliefs about sex, work, or morality. When you find yourself asserting a belief, ask yourself why you believe it. Why do you feel so strongly about it, and how does it connect with your values? Does the belief make sense to you when you break it down? Does the belief hold you back, or does it empower you? Does it make you feel an unacceptable emotion? Why is that emotion unacceptable?

Is it realistic?

Does it apply to your whole life and not just some instances?

What if you believed the opposite? Why is that so bad? Why do you find the opposite belief wrong? Is it wrong or is it just a preference? How do you feel about those who hold different beliefs? Question everything and make sure that you're not indoctrinated. Some beliefs are so ingrained into our psyche that we can't remember why we started believing them in the first place.

The point is to reclaim ownership of your life; to do that, you have to reclaim ownership of your *mind*.

Liz is a corporate dropout turned lifestyle designer and pithy personal development blogger. She's also the Community & Operations Manager at Live Your Legend. To find out more, go to her blog at A Life on Your Terms and download her exclusive members-only Life Lovers Guide to the Galaxy. You can also find her on twitter at @elizabethseda. - See more at:

liveyourlegend.net/how-to-create-your-ultimate-maste rmind-group-workbook/#sthash.BlzK7GNg.dpuf

How You Can Stop Just Going through the Motions and Start Living the Life You Really Want
with Sibyl Chavis

"It's impossible ... said pride. It's risky ... said experience. It's pointless ... said reason. Just try and believe ... whispered the heart."
- Author Unknown

Wouldn't you say that one of the most frustrating things is to know that you **want "something more"** for your life and to feel that you **should be doing "something more"** BUT you don't specifically know everything you should be doing to get it?

And, on top of not knowing, you've got things today that must be handled – responsibilities, issues, people who rely on you and a litany of things that must be taken care of.

I didn't realize how common this trap was until I admitted to myself that I was in the trap. And, when I finally started telling other people, so many would *echoed the same sentiments.* That's when I figured out that many of us really are in the same boat and have found ourselves in this trap at one point or another in life.

Personally, I know I always wanted to believe that one day –somehow, someway – *I would find my way to "something more."* I was also very aware that for whatever reason, I hadn't really been doing enough of the right things to actually get me somewhere other than where I was.

It's not that I wasn't grateful for all that I did have, but somehow I had fallen into the trap I had always been warned about. I was on the "human hamster wheel" and on most days I was just going through the motions and doing my best to keep up with the daily grind.

Although, many of us have found ourselves in this position, where it finally dawns on you that you're in a place that you don't really want to be, *some will decide "it is what is" and stay stuck;* but other people will decide that they have to do *whatever they possibly can to get unstuck.*

So, I went for getting "unstuck" because I knew I couldn't live with the feeling that there was "something more" for the rest of my life. That feeling had really taken a toll on me and I knew I was being pushed closer and closer to a breaking point.

The reality is that when we reach this point, there really is only one question to answer … ***Do you want to stay where you are or have you finally reached the point where you just can't take it anymore and you are willing to do something about it <u>every single day</u> until you get to where you really want to be?***

That really is the only question to answer and once you decide your answer, the two paths ahead of you are very clear and distinct from one another. You know exactly what must be done.

If you choose to stay stuck in the hamster wheel or decide there's not anything you can really do about it:

• Simply keep doing what you've been doing. Stay on autopilot. Grind away day after day. Or,

If you choose it's time to find your way to your "something more" and live the life you really want to be living:

• Take advantage of the possibility you have every single day to take a step forward. Commit to doing at least one thing until you get to where you want to be.

It really is that black and white, and thankfully the choice is ours to make. We have all the control.

I think one of the most important things I've ever learned is that if there is something you've dreamed about or something more you want for your life, or even if you don't know what's wrong, but you know something is "off", then *you've got everything you need within you* to change it. You've just got to be honest with yourself, admit the status quo is not good enough and choose to change it.

Will you have to take continual steps day after day? Yes.

Will challenges arise and on some days will you be tired and not feel like pushing? Most likely.

Will you reach your "something more" and finally live the life you've always imagined for yourself? Absolutely … as long as you choose today (and every today that follows) to take another step forward until things fall into place and you get to where you really want to be.

The choice is yours. And, considering that you've read this far, it's probably time to go and get your "something more". It's not always about waiting for the perfect time, but realizing **you can make Now the perfect time.**

The Possibility of Today: Choosing to go and get your "Something More"

1. Rethink What Is Really Possible. Take 30 minutes, grab a piece of paper and write down what you really want. What is your "something more"? What feels most right for you?

2. Plant the Possibility Spiral Firmly In Your Mind. Remind yourself about the way things actually come together. In order to get where you want to be, you have to commit to take a continual step forward, push through challenges, learn whatever lessons you need to and keep going up your possibility spiral until you reach the top.

3. Get Organized & Take Action. Put together a list of at least 5-10 steps you can take in the next 30 days to move forward. Do at least one thing every day. Follow the same process every month until you get to where you want to be.

4. Meet Your Extraordinary Side. Tap into that place inside you, your Higher Self, the part of you that knows your true strength. As you move through the day, stay continually connected to your Extraordinary Side and let it flow into your work, your thoughts and your actions. When you feel like you're tired or you want to stop, connect to the feeling of your Extraordinary Side.

Live Today Better than Yesterday.

Sibyl Chavis is a Harvard-trained lawyer who left the lucrative corporate world on the East coast to create a life of greater clarity and purpose. Formerly in practice at a leading law firm and then Executive Vice President for HR at a multicultural advertising agency, she now is a writer. She is currently writing her second book and she also writes "The Possibility of Today" (www.possibilityoftoday.com) an online magazine focused on providing simple tips for Living Today Better than Yesterday. She lives in Pasadena, CA with her husband and two children.

Spreading a Message
with Amy Clover

Every single one of us has a movement inside that's just aching to get out. However, the process of harnessing that inner movement to create a tangible, effective message to spread to the world is easier said than done.

I created this movement from my personal story. What I fought against for years, is now my driving force. My fight with clinical depression and suicidal thoughts drove me to find fitness as an outlet, and now I am passionate about helping others find their own outlets so that they can shed their light on the world.

The lack of support and hope I experienced while I was in the darkness was my motivation to create this project. Now, I want to start talking about how you can do the same.

You are living your story. Everything you've been through up until now has made you who you are, and has given you a drive to help others.

Believing that you are capable of creating massive change is crucial to creating a movement. You have earned this right to help other people overcome their setbacks simply because you are alive and breathing today.

You don't need to be deemed "special" or "chosen."

You choose your own life, and I highly suggest you opt for an epic one.
So why devote yourself to helping others?

Our intrinsic need as human beings, to serve others, is the factor that is often forgotten in the complete picture of happiness. By devoting ourselves to altruistic goals, we actually help ourselves. We feel more confident, fulfilled and useful when we can help others. It completes the mind, body, spirit spectrum that I believe is so important to achieving complete happiness.

Still with me? Cool, let's get this movement started. Here are the three steps to get you from story to movement and start spreading your message far and wide:

1. What's your story? What speaks to you?

What causes are you passionate about, either from personal experience or from a point of empathy? The causes that speak most directly to you at your core are the ones to focus on here. Those issues that make you emotional, *that make you want to get up and fight*, are the ones to hone in on.

Jot down causes or issues that speak to you in the deepest sense.

2. How can you help?

How can you use your unique skill set to help fill that void?

You are completely unique, my friend. How can you utilize your personal tool belt to help others out there in the world?

Be creative. Venture outside of the box with ideas. There are no wrong answers.

Take out a journal and brainstorm all the possible ways you can approach this idea. You can't dream too big here.

3. Act & Amplify

Now that you have your ideas in place, it's time to take action.

Divide your big goal into mini ones. Take one at a time to avoid getting overwhelmed by the enormity of the change you wish to create.

Do not be afraid to scream your message from the rooftops. If you don't, who will?
Movements are made by people who aren't afraid to fight for them. If you want to be a movement-maker, you have to live loud. You first have to let people know that the issue needs to be addressed, and then offer a resolution.

The clearer you are with your message, and the more precise instructions you give people, the more adamant they will be about offering their assistance and support to boost your movement to world-changing levels.

<u>Tell people:</u>
What exactly you hope to achieve
How you're going to do it
How they can help

In the end, it's totally up to you whether you choose to create a movement or not. I just know from personal experience that I never felt this whole and full of life before finding my calling, and I sincerely wish for you to have that, too.

Happy moving.

Amy Clover is the voice behind Strong Inside Out and The 30x30 Project tour and movement. She aims to inspire hope through movement with her tour across North America of donation-based boot camps and meetups to bring awareness and funds to the suicide prevention nonprofit, To Write Love On Her Arms.

Section Four: Connection

Who Will Take Out the Garbage?
with Charles Eisenstein

Charles allowed me to include this. He talks about a world where everyone is doing the work they love by following their passions. He also goes on to give ideas on how to deal with the less meaningful work.

Enter Charles...

I had a conversation today about the beautiful world that I believe will be born out of the converging crises of our age.

One characteristic of this world is that each person will have recovered a very basic, simple birthright: to wake up in the morning excited and happy about their work for the day. We will be in love with what we do; in other words, we will all be artists.

Everybody has probably experienced this feeling at one time or another; the feeling of being passionately involved in a creative project.

That passion is the sign of what might be called authentic work, true work, or soul work. The human spirit rebels at doing anything we don't truly care about.

This rebellion is closest to the surface in the young: hence, the sullen, resentful, rebellious, angry teenager. As we get older and the spirit crumbles, we come to accept that life is "just like that." We grow accustomed to working drudgingly in pursuit of external rewards, doing what we love only during our "time off." Think of the assumptions built into that infamous phrase, "time off."

Time off from what?

If we enjoy freedom only on the weekends, vacations, and evenings of our lives, then what does that say about the rest of life? It is slavery. What about being free all the time? Freedom is a reality when you do something you love. You are free.

I am not just speaking of the obvious drudgery of the working class here. Even among the elite, many occupations are not rewarding on their own merits.

One corporate executive told me that his job consisted of "lying to the customer." Another told me that his job was to scare customers into buying computer security systems that they didn't actually need. And imagine if your job were to promote

Colgate over Crest, or Pepsi over Coke, or any brand over another, essentially identical brand.

Consider if your job was to write software to help someone else promote a product that no one really needed. Or to provide the financing or insurance for someone to promote a product that is unnecessary. Something in you would say, "I was not put here on earth to sell soda. I was not made to lie to the customer. I am not meant to make children learn standardized testing curricula. My purpose on earth is not to push a broom. I am not intended to fill out medical billing statements. I was not put here on earth to collect garbage."

The nature of work-as-we-know-it—tedious, routine, degrading to self or others, unfulfilling to the spirit—has very deep roots. One root grows from the Machine, with its requirement for standardized, replaceable parts and processes. Another grows from the mentality of domestication, laboring daily for the sake of a future harvest.

Ultimately, all of these ideologies originate from our sense of self as discrete and separate. More for me is less for you. The true artist never does anything merely "good enough"—good enough for the grade, for the customer, for the boss.

The true artist keeps works tediously on a project until he or she can look upon it with satisfaction. Then, and only then, is it ready to give to the universe.

The true artist might receive money for their work, but the work is not done *for* the money because no amount of money is sufficient. The real motivation is elsewhere. True art is beyond price.

My conversation partner asked, "But in such a world, who will collect the garbage?" My short answer was, "In a more beautiful world, we are not going to produce very much garbage!" Now I would like to give a longer answer.

Both the question and the answer were spoken on two levels, the first literal, and the second metaphoric. On the literal level, we can envision an economic and monetary system that structurally discourages waste.

When all costs are internalized, a huge incentive is created to produce goods that are fully reusable or recyclable.

This concept is a return to the very recent past. My ex-wife recalls that during her childhood in rural Taiwan, there was no such thing as a garbage truck. Food scraps were composted or fed to the pigs.

Newspaper, metal, and glass were all recycled. Food bought at the market was taken home wrapped in bamboo leaves. Containers were refilled by local distributors or producers. Another friend of mine recently returned from a visit to Cuba, where she was amazed to find that an entire village of several hundred people only filled one garbage can per week.

Ultimately, to make an object beautifully requires that we consider its entire history and future. The artist-engineers of a more beautiful world will incorporate reusability and sustainability into their design specs. They will do so for beauty's sake, for their own joy and satisfaction, and for an economic incentive. Products that generate waste will be more expensive.

Beauty and money will no longer be at odds. If you are curious to know more, read the economics of Paul Hawken and Amory Lovins, as well as Chapter seven of The Ascent of Humanity.

But really, the question is about more than just garbage. Generalized, it might go something like this:

"There are a certain number of unpleasant, tedious, degrading tasks that have to get done in order to have a modern society. Who will do these

tasks in a world where everyone insists on work that is rewarding?"

My answer is general. Menial tasks will become much less necessary if industrial design consciously seeks, not to minimize costs, but rather to minimize drudgery, tedium, and waste. Secondly, our demand for endless piles of cheap, generic consumer items will diminish as we transition into a new conception of wealth and surround ourselves with durable, elegant material objects made with love.

I believe that many consumer goods that are mass-produced today will revert back to local, more labor-intensive production. This is especially true of food, and also to some extent clothing, medicine, shelter, and entertainment. Thirdly, as new currency systems render money into a less scarce commodity, we will no longer support enterprises whose dominant motivation is to reduce costs and maximize dollar efficiency.

We will desire goods and services produced by artists, not slaves. A garment made in a sweatshop will seem ugly and repugnant to us. To have a surfeit of such things is a strange concept of wealth indeed.

To me, true wealth would be to live among unique treasures, not mass-produced uniform objects made with the crass motive of profit above all.

In a more beautiful world, we will not be comfortable eating at restaurants or staying at hotels or working in office buildings that depend logistically on masses of broken souls pushing mops, washing dishes, flipping burgers, and entering data. Nor will there be many people sufficiently broken, by training or poverty, to do such work. Any enterprise will have to make consideration for human dignity.

I believe there will still be such things as hotels and restaurants in a more beautiful world, and there will still be a limited amount of work washing dishes and chopping vegetables and pushing mops. These jobs are really only degrading and soul-destroying when you feel compelled to do them day in and day out, with no hope of anything better. For a teenager to do something like this a few hours a week for a year or two is a different matter entirely.

One of the best jobs I ever had was in a cafeteria dish room in college. There are times in life as well, personal transitions for instance, during which a period of mindless labor can be comforting. So there may always be a limited place for such jobs in even the most beautiful society. The difference is that no one will feel stuck in such a position.

People will do many more things for themselves. It is degrading to clean other people's toilets all day; it is not degrading to clean your own toilet, or even another person's toilet out of love. I do not find it degrading to change my son's diapers, or to physically care for an ill loved one.

Such tasks are part of the richness of life, yet ironically, in the supposedly richest society on Earth, we pay other people to perform the tasks of daily living, converting them from richness to degradation. I think that the toilets in tomorrow's office buildings will be cleaned by the people who work there.

All the same, it is nice to be pampered sometimes, and there are people who love to do that for others.

A more beautiful world will abound in inns, restaurants, spas, massage clinics, and other places devoted to making people feel great. Inns and restaurants will operate on a smaller scale than today's mega-hotels, and all the slogans about personalized hospitality will come true.

There are some who say that if everyone suddenly insisted on doing only rewarding work, and refused to compromise their dignity, then society as we know it would fall apart.

From this assumption follow a regime of oppression and control, with the associated guilt of knowing that one person's freedom and fulfillment is based upon another's slavery and misery.

Well, this way of thinking is correct about one thing: Society as we know it would indeed fall apart. But that doesn't mean a descent to barbarism. In fact, I doubt the transition would be nearly as difficult as you might imagine if, say, all the garbage collectors of the world went on permanent holiday.

Our purchasing habits, our composting habits, and so on would change very quickly; I am sure, soon to be followed by our production systems.

If all the mop-pushers quit, saying, *"I'm too good for this"*; if all the burger-flippers quit, saying, *"I am too good for this"*; if all the marketers decided that lying were beneath their dignity, if all the soldiers said, *"I will no longer kill"*; if all the manufacturers said, *"I will no longer produce in a way that pollutes the air"*; if everyone just refused to go along with anything that felt wrong, can you imagine the world we could create?

Let us not be afraid to create a world in which no one is broken to be anything less than an artist.

I think we can all begin creating a world like that right now. We can become refusers ourselves, as much as courage allows, and we can encourage each other with the knowledge, "You are meant to do something beautiful here."

Most of all, we can see in every maid, every check-out cashier, every janitor, ever data drone, a divinely creative spirit that is much bigger than that role.

See everyone as big. Never through word or deed imply that they are small. Every time you treat one of the lowest functionaries of our society with humanity and respect, you are committing a small, revolutionary act, because your respect contradicts what the system has made them.

Even if they are 99 percent broken to their role, even if they accept with 99 percent of their being that life is just like this, even if they willingly comply with their own degradation, there is something deep down that refuses to ever accept it.

No human spirit can ever truly be broken. Your humanity and respect will speak to that tiny, buried, and indomitable spark of dignity and rebellion in every human soul.

Charles Eisenstein is an author and public speaker, and self-described "degrowth activist". He is the author of several books including The Ascent of Humanity *and* Sacred Economics.

An Individual Development Plan for Following Your Passions

You're on the brink of something new but don't know where to begin.

Life brings new possibilities to the forefront of your thoughts on a regular basis.

Most seem to be wishful thinking and some become something more.

A light bulb of inspiration sweeps you off your feet for a moment.

But then what happens?

You let it slide out of your thoughts as you continue with your daily routine.

Ideas come and go, some good, some bad. These ideas are nothing more than little desires. The ones that we notice and take a hold of are those that have better potential to move us. They lead us to ponder other possibilities for our lives.

Remember, we're talking about trying to unearth your passions and learning to recognize the ones of most importance to you. Sometimes it can be difficult to recall what you are passionate about, outside of your everyday life, family, routines, job, money, worry, debt, yada, yada, yada.

I thought of some good ideas that seem to help me when I just can't figure it out. Ways to bring about the passionate, creative side of ourselves, so that we can dare to dream again. Notice how I said, again?

We have all been through it before. Once upon a time or another, you have had a dream. A dream of something that would make you happy. **Something that would bring you joy and fulfillment.**

Most of the time, this dream is lost during adolescence, but that deep fire still burns, and from time to time, it lets its presence feel known and throws you a desire that gets your blood pumping. Once again, this is usually the point that you let it slip away, taking it as nothing more than a *"what if"*, or just plain old unrealistic.

That's when you need to stop yourself, refocus, regain some inspiration, and continue on your path. The world is yours for the making, so don't let the fear of the unknown, or the consensus of the majority, manage your decisions and your thoughts. Doing that would essentially be enslaving yourself to a system that defines what is and what isn't possible.

Sure, some things may seem impossible, but the universe is giving by nature. Those that know what they are worth, that humans are capable of much more than they realize, understand that action yields results. Daydreaming is good for the imagination, but taking action on your ideas is the only way to know whether something is possible.

Below are some ideas to gaining focus and clarity in pursuit of your passions.

Find Your Focus

It's super easy to become distracted with the variety of circumstances surrounding your everyday life. When a new idea comes along that you want to pursue, you often lose focus because of those circumstances.

These circumstances might include the following: **a dreadful job, household chores, television, video games, bills, and other daily rituals that slow your mind's progression.**

Everyday life can take up enough time on its own – add in the time wasted indulging in the entertainment of modern society what time is left for your real purpose? Life purpose presents itself to you in the form of your aspirations and desires. The true desires that come from inside you end up being forced down beneath the present moment.

I have found I can change this cycle of mind slavery, by finding my focus. Try to hold on to an idea that surfaces and run with it. Maybe it will be worth pursuing and perhaps not, but if you ignore it, you will never know. When you focus on a promising idea, it has a chance at becoming something more, an act.

The actions that are worth pursuing are the ones that require your focus. Work on developing your focus. Jot down your hopes and reasoning for holding on to an idea. Why do you desire it? Is it an idea worth pursuing? Do you have a passion for it? Will it make you happy? Could it change your life?

You never know when "*The Idea*" will come to you. Without the proper focus necessary for taking action, it will simply pass you by. A thousand ideas will come and go.

One idea is all it takes to change your world.
Try To Find Clarity
In a world where our days are full and our stress levels at an all-time high, it is crucial that you find

clarity in your own life. With clarity comes insight, which brings passion and pleasure to your mind. When you find clarity in what you really want in life and in the ideas you have, you can find yourself in a better, happier place mentally.

Clarity starts with recognizing that you are more than what you do. You have more to offer than what others think. Each and every one of us has the potential of achieving something magnificent. Clearing your mind of the clutter and pursing your own unique ideas will show you what you are capable of.

When your mind is clear and you allow yourself to listen to your heart, the gateway of unlimited possibilities awakens and will shine through. If you want to find clarity, you must let go.

Let Go Of Fear

Let go of the constraints that bind you. When you listen to your heart and allow your true self to emerge, you are able to let go of the fears that follow. Let go of the fear of thinking that an idea is ridiculous, that it could never happen, that you are not good enough, that you are not capable, and that seemingly inevitable fear of the unknown.

We often get too accustomed to our routines. The fear of leaving our comfort zone and venturing out into the unknown can be powerful. You need to let go of the mindset that you are too busy, too broke, too tired, or too lazy. Just follow through with something new, and you will be glad you did afterwards. Even if it ended up being a stupid idea, at least you opened the door to taking action in the future.

When I decided to start Unplugged Recreated, I was afraid that others wouldn't understand or care what I had to say. I didn't think I was a good enough writer (still don't), but I let go of those fears because I knew it was my passion to help others see that there is another way of living.

A way to live life without being told what to do and how to do it. My passion for writing and helping others has shown through with my strong desire to change the world. I am still afraid that no one will ever read this. That I am writing to the mirror. You know what? That's okay. I am all right with that because I love to talk about these things.

I don't really have many people in my day-to-day life that share my passions, but you know what? As long as I have a computer and a keyboard, I don't care. I have you, even if you *is* the mirror. You get my point. As long as you love what you do, just do it.

Keep Moving Forward

I'll let you in on a little secret. I have no idea what I am doing. I really don't. All of the topics and ideas that are part of Unplugged Recreated are not my own. Some days, I am not sure I am bringing anything new to the table. Of course, I am not copying others words and plagiarizing them or anything along those lines. But I assure you, I am not the first one with these ideas, values, and messages.

I'll tell you another secret. I don't care. I know that the information I have has already been covered in some way. That doesn't bother me because I know that it is what I love to teach and the way I teach it is unique to me. I love to read about these topics and I believe in what they stand for. I believe that we can change *the* world, while changing *our* world, and I want to share it with you.

I don't consider it wrong. I think of it as passing the torch. By using my own voice, I am basically relaying information to you. How would I have discovered a topic I cared about, if it weren't for someone else sharing it? In a similar way, how would they have been able to share their view of the same topic, if it weren't for someone else?

I am not intending to call anyone a copycat, because they're not and I'm not. We are just spreading the message so that everyone has a chance at finding it.

That's my secret. Do your best to find your passion, and when you find it, run with it. Remove the distractions, focus on your passion, and take action. Seek clarity and keep moving forward.

Human Connection is the Key to Freedom

A dream you dream alone is only a dream. A dream you dream together is reality".
-John Lennon

There is a time in our life when we start to understand more about ourselves and the life we live. We begin to understand just what it takes to be happy and realize that life is not about us; rather, it is about our relationships with others.

If we're lucky, we figure this out before we become so consumed with our own wants and needs, that we sacrifice our connections with others in the process.

To understand why it is not about us, but about others, we must look deep inside our own thoughts and desires. Those of us who seek to constantly improve, chase our dreams, and dare to desire unknown possibilities, will eventually discover that the connections we make with others is the most integral missing piece of our lives.

The piece that, although at first is unwanted due to reasons like fear, doubt, and selfishness, is the very one that leads us to the attainment of our elusive goals. Human connection is the key that unlocks almost every door on our journeys.

Reaching For Your Dreams

It's a long road; your path to freedom. But if you can find a shortcut or two, without sacrificing your integrity, won't you take it? Of course, it takes a long enough time trying to come to grips with what your dream is (at least it did for me), let alone know how to pursue it. Or to even build up the courage to take the **first steps**. So what do you do?

Build Relationships

If you are more of an introvert (like myself), you are more comfortable doing things by yourself and don't necessarily feel at ease approaching others and asking for help. Here's a little advice that took me too long to learn: Overcome the fear of connecting with others, because it will save you a lot of time and effort.

You are already connecting with people every day through your search for answers. Especially because it is with others that you find everything you need to complete your path to personal freedom. You may not speak with them directly, but you are taking their advice and putting it to use. They are helping you already, you just need to take the next step and approach them directly. Here are some tips on doing just that.

- *Become a member of their community*
- *Send them an e-mail, introducing yourself as a member of their tribe*
- *Participate in the community by interacting in the comments*
- *Interact with them on social media places like Twitter, Facebook, and Google Plus*
- *Ask them for help or advice. If they say no, that's okay. Try again later and move on.*
- *Provide them with the value that you bring to the community. You have it. Don't be afraid to show it*
- *Don't be one and done. Build relationships that last.*
- *Be genuine. Don't be the guy or gal that is out for only self-benefit.*
- *Become a friend because real friends don't use each other, they share.*
- *Help others that come to you.*

The people that you want to make connections with are those that are never too busy to respond to someone who approaches them. This doesn't mean that I will respond to every Tweet or e-mail I am sent, but generally, if someone sends me a genuine message and gives me a reason to respond, I do. It may take a few days, but I get back to almost everyone.

Using Human Connection for Your Freedom

As I mentioned earlier, human connection is the key to unlock every door on your journey to freedom. So how exactly do you use the key and which doors do you open?

Discovering the answer to this question took me a ton of time and research. When I was first starting my journey, I found myself randomly browsing through areas that interested me. I looked up information on how to become free, how to follow my passions, and tried to figure out which ways would be best for me. I had to find the trustworthy information and rule out get-rich-quick scams.

Over time, I started to figure out who was legit and which information sources have the answers I was seeking. I struggled, I quit, I learned, I fell on my face; I gained experience, I learned more, I taught other, I gave of myself, and I began to change. This was my journey and it can be yours too if you want it. It is a little more detailed than this, but this description is essentially the path.

The amount of time it takes and the number of times we fail depends on how we learn, what we do, and most importantly, who we know. It's almost impossible to survive a journey if you don't gain help along the way. You need to make connections. Have I said that before? I'll repeat it for good measure. You need to make connections.

It's hard to understand, rather, subconsciously we don't want to understand, that the one thing stopping us from moving forward is the inability to connect with others in our environment. I heard this saying once: "Be everywhere."

It stuck with me. I interpret that statement as, "reach out to as many people as you can, in your environment, even if you have doubts. You need to take action, so just do it."

What is Stopping You?

I'm not sure it is the same for everyone, but for me, it was fear that stopped me in my tracks. Fear was an obstacle on my path to freedom; an obstacle that stalled my effort to do what I knew had to be done to get to where I wanted to be. I was scared that I wasn't ready, that I would be rejected, that I wasn't good enough.

Know what I discovered? That it wasn't about me. My fear was trying to convince me to resist connecting with others, out of selfish reasons. Look. You have to get past the "I'm not good enough noise". It is the biggest B.S. in the world. We are all human, we act human, with values, morals, and a heart (most of us anyway), so being star struck is just ridiculous.

I say, you need to just start taking action and interacting with everyone in your field, niche, environment, tribe, community, small army, or whatever you want to call it. You need to dive in, e-mail, comment, give compliments (don't brown nose), guest post, tweet, like, plus, YouTube, interview, attend, involve yourself, and be genuine.

As with any adventure to finding one's freedom, there are lessons learned, experiences held, battles won and lost, mistakes made and fixed, but the one key element holds true. If you build connections, develop relationships, and give and receive support, you will eventually succeed.

Human connection is the inspiration that grabs you, the motivation that pulls you, and the help that moves you forward. Make enough connections and you will have all you need to follow through with your dreams.

How Connection Turns the Impossible into an Obtainable Force

Once in a great while, a movement begins. This can be an idea or theory for improvement or a better way to do something, a new way to view the world, to make a change, to help others, to help ourselves.

Relationships and connectivity are ultimately what make the world a better place. It's the connection with others who hold similar beliefs and values to our own that make a good idea become *great*. The more people connected to an idea, the more powerful it becomes.

I didn't always believe that. I used to think that I could do anything and do it on my own. I thought life was mine for the taking and that others were holding me back. Of course, I believed that I could still persevere; it was just going to be more difficult. I can't tell you how naive and wrong I was in my thinking.

It's the Connection that binds us

I've said this many times, but it truly is the connection with others that can make anything possible. For example, when millions of people come together for a certain cause or idea, it is the connection, the beliefs, and the values that they share are that make them so powerful. When we connect with those around us, we become better versions of ourselves.

When we connect with others, we become part of a community. When a community connects with other communities, the strength of human connection becomes exponentially significant. True transformation is a result of the connections of millions of people focused around a certain belief, value, or idea.

There is nothing that can't be done with the power of human connection. Period.

Reasons for Connecting

The reasons why we connect with others are not nearly as important as what we achieve as result. Like anything in life, the power of human connection can be used either for the greater good, or for the continued evil of this world.

The most powerful form of connection should be one that unites humankind, in order to bring about greater change in the world. Connections created with the goal of igniting positive change in our world, are the connections that make a lasting and fulfilling impact.

When you're working toward something that benefits everyone, you are ultimately benefiting yourself. This brings fulfillment and joy into your life, the lives of others, and the world around you.

Making the Impossible, Possible

The knowledge that human connection is one of the keys to unlimited possibilities is only good if you utilize it. Connections can come in many forms, so it isn't just making them that's useful. You need to learn how to use the connections for the benefit of what you're aiming for. Whether it's coming together with others in your environment to support a cause or making the connections you need for overcoming obstacles on your path, there is a common recipe for establishing these connections.

Reach Out

You can't make connections if no one knows who you are. Reach out to the people in your environment. Offer them help, be supportive of what they are doing, and become an active member of their community.

I always email the people whom I mention on my blog. I am not pushy or looking for favors. I give them thanks for what they are doing and sometimes ask a brief question. If you show them support, more than likely they will show you support as well.

Keep it Simple

We get so caught up with who we are and what others think of us, we often don't realize how drastically we unnecessarily complicate things. I don't know how long I waited to approach the people in my community, for fear of rejection, being ignored, or not being good enough.

That's just ridiculous when you really think about it. Make things simple. You're a person, they're a person. We're all just people trying to make it in the world.

Don't get caught up in the celebrity hoopla. Just keep it simple. It's just life.

Be Yourself

"To be yourself is all that you can do,"
- Audioslave

Be authentic. Be genuine in what you do. When making connections with others, don't be the guy/girl that comes off as someone you're not. Being genuine also means being consistent in the way you act. This also goes back to not caring too much about what others think of you. Be yourself and don't worry about it.

Be Persistent, but not Pushy

So you've done everything you know how. You have reached out to someone you want to make a connection with. You commented on their blog, re-tweeted, Facebook liked, and sent them an email showing your support. You decide to reach out to either offer help or get advice, or maybe you wish to be a guest author on their blog. You get no response.

What do you do?

Listen. Not everyone will respond to you. Depending on who you are trying to connect with, they may get hundreds of emails a day. There is no way to keep up with that. If you have done enough to become noticed, you may get a response or you might not. Don't give up and move onto someone else just yet. Give them a week and try again. Give them another week then try again. If you don't hear anything back after the third email, you need to either rethink your strategy or who you are trying to make connections with.

   *A little advice… Start making connections with up-and-comers first. It's harder to connect with A-listers who have thousands of subscribers if you are still "a nobody". Good news is that they were also new at one point in time. It takes time, effort, and persistence. Just don't be pushy or you'll come off as selfish.

Be Confident

Let your confidence show. You don't want to be cocky, but you also don't want to show a lack of self-esteem. So don't beg, and don't expect something to happen. Just be confident in your abilities and show it in an authentic way. Simple, right?

Keep on Keepin' On

Joe dirt kept going, no matter what life threw at him. You should do the same. Progress doesn't happen if you're not moving forward. Life is always moving us forward. It's the pace you choose that will make the difference in your life. Be inspired to make a difference and use the connections with others to get there. All you can do is give it your all. So go get it and make some friends while you're at it.

Lifestyle Design: Recreate, Restructure, Redesign Your Life

Have you ever wondered what your life would have been like if you would have just done that one thing?

Have you thought that if you would have started when you had the chance, you might have been able to make your life dreams come true?

If you're like me, you're not alone. Actually, if you haven't had questions similar to these, then you are obviously a very successful and fulfilled individual and I could not congratulate you more.

Why Didn't We Start Earlier?

See, we go through life doing what we have to do. Doing what our brains processes tell us to do, based on our human needs. There are four basic needs that all of us need to meet, all the time.

We do what it takes to have certainty in our lives. We need to have security and have a need for survival. On that same note, we all have a need to have some uncertainty and the need to be safe, yet have some excitement and be spontaneous.

Everyone has a need to be significant, a need to have a sense of self, and a need to matter.

Finally, we all have a need for connection. For love. To have someone to be intimate with. To have friends and people with whom we can bond and share our lives. These four human needs are in all of us. Some of us feel a lack in certain areas, yet all of us are constantly moving toward fulfilling these needs.

The thing is this: we view these needs based on how we perceive the world around us. What does it mean to have certainty?

What do we do that will meet these needs? For most of us, it means living a life much similar to the lives of others. Doing what we know has worked for millions of other people for generations.

That's also the problem. What has worked for generations and has been the norm for millions, isn't working so great anymore. What was once certain isn't as certain anymore.

The world has changed, society has changed, and so has the way we live. We are at the end of an era, the brink of a radical transformation.

There is a **new economy** on the rise. One that enables us to truly transform our lives. The ways of the former society have grown outdated and there is something new on the horizon.

If you are not yet aware of this new economy, you are probably still struggling through life, doing whatever you have to in order to get by, even if you don't like it. I'm here to help you see the new path. I'm here to give you hope.

There is a new way of doing things in this evolving world. You don't have to struggle and merely *wonder* what tomorrow will hold. You can *discover* a new tomorrow.

You can build a life for yourself in this new economy that allows you to live comfortably. A life that allows you to start living the life that you want. A life that gives you the freedom, security, and fulfillment that you could only dream of in the past.

I'm here to tell you that your dreams are not mere dreams; they have the potential to become your reality.

Once you are informed, educated, and ready to take action, you are on your way to building a new life for yourself and your family. To building a lifestyle design your way.

What it Takes

You know the feeling that you get when you see something **epic** happen. It could be a great movie where the underdog overcomes.

Maybe it's game six of the World Series and your favorite team, against all odds, triumphs in victory. A sense of euphoria overcomes you. Once it happens, you feel fulfilled. You feel like anything is possible.

Unfortunately, the feeling goes away. As much as you are in the moment, the moment fades. Soon afterwards, you return to *"reality"* and your life goes on.

What if you could make that kind of feeling last? Do you think it's possible? Why or why not?

Now, I'm not sure that you can make that intense feeling of the moment last, because let's face it, moments are by nature, fleeting. However, I believe that the inspiration for these moments is possible for all of us. You can be the underdog. You can be the one who overcomes the greatest of obstacles, in order to reach incredible heights.

Of course, it isn't as easy as it is to imagine, is it?

That's why all of us aren't living these stories.

But, why not? Because it's not possible?

That's what a lot of people think.

Because you don't have the talent or natural ability?

Nope. All things can be learned.

It has a lot to do with the society we live in, the environment that surrounds us, and what we have been taught. But, the great part about life is that anything can change in an instant. Fortunately for you, you have found your way to this article.
There is a way to find your way to the top of your mountain. To make your dreams come alive where fulfillment comes in like waves on a white sandy beach. You just have to do what it takes.

The Plan

Maybe you have heard of this formula before, maybe not. You create a new plan for your life that goes against the conventional way of doing things.
You find what you're passionate about, *build a business* around it, while spreading a message and making a difference in the world.

You build a comfortable life for yourself now versus waiting 50 years until you retire, hoping that you have the energy and health to do what you really want. Not to mention, hoping to have the 401k account to make it happen.

Sometimes this approach is called lifestyle design. I just call it living your passion or becoming an entrepreneur.

The idea is to be fulfilled in what you do while helping others, spreading a message to the world, and making a comfortable income to do the things you should be able to do in life.

Why aren't you doing it?

Being an entrepreneur may not be for everyone. But if it's something you have said you want but you aren't doing it, ask yourself why not? It's clearly a proven and attainable goal in this new economy. Don't worry, I get it. It's hard. It takes time, work, and effort to get going especially when you don't even know how long it will take or whether you will succeed.

Yes, it does take time. Yes, it does take a ton of effort and work. And yes, if you're not sure you will succeed you probably won't. **So what do you do?**

Recreate, Restructure, & Redesign Your Life

We're only people. As human beings, we need to learn before we can do. We learn best when we have a system in place to help us put all the information together. Not everyone has the same way of learning, but we can learn and implement what we know much easier when we follow a specific framework.

There are many different types of frameworks for many different topics. Even the Lifestyle Design field has different frameworks built by those experts who have done it before. I have put together a framework that will allow you to learn the information that you need to find, start, and run a lifestyle design business.

I have discovered that it is easier (*for me at least*), to start with a basic idea that is easy to remember and then break it down into baby steps.

Today, I give you the idea that will be the structure of the framework that I have learned and implemented into my own business.

The idea is simple. **Recreate, Restructure, & Redesign Your Life.**

I use the same structure when I talk about my message of making a change in our world. This structure relates to a message.

The message is to recreate your life so that it aligns with your dreams, passions, and message to the world.

Restructure your life so that you are able to believe, learn, and enable yourself to follow through. Finally, redesign your life by taking action on the lifestyle design you want for yourself. **Sounds simple, right?**

Well, the idea is simple, but putting it into action can be much more complicated. Don't let the fear of failure intimidate you. Just keep in mind that if you want to achieve this, it will take a lot of desire, effort, and hard work.

Section Five:
Dream Design

Dreaming Big
with Natalie Sisson

We all have a dream. Some grand vision we'd love to see come to fruition one day. Something that scares us yet compels us and energizes us at the same time.

So why is it that so many people seem to put those dreams in a box and shelve them away for a day that never comes?

It's tragic to think of all those boxed up dreams, slowly dying away, deprived of oxygen and never likely to see the light of day. I don't want to see that happen anymore.

My mission in life is to get you to court bolder dreams and make them a reality,

The two most common excuses I hear for not making your dreams come true are:

- Your natural inherent fears of failure (or success)
- Lack of time and money to make it happen.

So let's tackle these right now. Below I share my strategies for moving past fear and your excuses of lack of time and money, as well as examples of how I did this.

Making your dreams a reality

Fear is natural, it's something we have to face anytime we are setting out to do something that is pushing us outside of our comfort zone or asking us to step up and take a risk.

You have to be willing to deal with fear and those feelings of discomfort to actually make change in your life, and more importantly, make those dreams come true.

When I set out to write The Suitcase Entrepreneur book I had a number of pretty major doubts, which included:

- Who am I to write a book and consider myself a leader in how to create freedom in business and adventure in life?
- I've never written a book how on earth am I going to achieve this?
- What if people hate what I write about and my book bombs and it ruins my reputation?

- This is going to be a big investment and what if none of it pays off and I lose money?

So how did I overcome this?

1. **Start by taking fear out to lunch**

   Sit down at the table, across from fear. Give it a name and have a frank conversation with it. Tell it why you're going to go ahead and do what you've set out to do. Then ask it to leave so you can continue to enjoy your lunch. Honestly this tactic works. Once you name your fear and treat it as a person or object you can deal with it more rationally and tell it where to go!

   Example: I sat at a table and worked through every single fear that was coming up in my head as if I was addressing a person seated across from me. They asked me the questions I had running through my head, and I answered with upmost confidence and belief that I was capable of doing this. Even if I didn't feel 100% certain, I acted as if I was and immediately felt way more capable that I could pull this off.

2. **Get comfortable with feeling uncomfortable**.
   The initial push back you'll receive when you're making change and working towards your dreams is this constant feeling of feeling uncomfortable. Learn to embrace this uncertainty and accept this feeling as part of the dynamics of the change and growth you're going through. Once you accept this you'll be better able to deal with it on a daily basis – and trust me you will feel this more often than you realize.

   Example: As I was writing my book, I'd have days when I felt totally in the flow and believed I was qualified to write this, that in fact I was a writer and that people would love this book. On other days nothing seemed to come out the way I wanted and I doubted my very ability to write anything of value for my readers.

3. **Surround yourself with a support network**
   When you have a big dream you're going to have to deal with your own inner critic and self-doubt, as well as that of others who just don't understand what you're trying to do. Usually this is well meaning friends and family who care for you, but project their fears on to you. Why are you listening to them? Tell them, "thank you for your concerns but right now I

need your support because I'm going to do this no matter what."

What matters is that YOU believe in what you're setting out to achieve and you make it happen no matter what. Learn how to manage these moments of fear and doubt. Look for what you can put in place to make it feel safe for you to move forward. A strong support network of friends, mentors and advisors is going to make it even easier for you to forge ahead.

Example: During the book writing process I had numerous Skype calls and in person meetings with friends who were published authors. I used them as a sounding board to talk about the challenges they faced and the solutions they came up with. They gave me little nuggets of wisdom and advice when I needed it most. They also made me feel that I was doing all the right things and kept me focused on the bigger picture (when I wasn't).

I also turned to my Kickstarter backers, and my online blog and social media community to enlist their support along the way. I did this by giving them snippets of the book writing journey and asking their opinion which was always overwhelmingly positive and made me realize this was a worthwhile dream to pursue.

I also had a few people tell me they didn't think I could do it, which only served to fuel my fire and make sure this was the best book I'd ever written. You need to learn to harness other peoples' fears and opinions to your advantage.

4. **Make a firm decision and set a date**.
There is no better way to deal with the fears that are keeping you stuck and the voice that screams "I don't know how to do this" than making a decision to take action. To make that even more real, you need to set a date by when you're going to achieve that action. Once you make this public you are asking your friends, community, and network to hold you accountable to do it. This means it's no longer just you doing this there's a whole bunch of people standing behind you, willing you to make your dreams come true.

   Example: I ran a Kickstarter crowd funding campaign to fund my self-publishing efforts and to make sure people supported my project and that my book should be written. I was thrilled when it was 120 percent funded by close to 200 people who believed in my book. What's more, I now had not only the money to self-publish, but all those people holding me accountable to complete the book and send them an advanced copy by the middle of July.

This absolutely worked like a charm as I am a woman of my word and did not want to let anyone down. As a result I wrote my book to meet this deadline and moved heaven and earth to make it a reality. Without this deadline, I may still be writing my book!

Remember, nothing worth doing in this lifetime is ever going to be easy or straightforward. If it was, then everybody would be doing it. Your dreams deserve to be fulfilled, no matter how long it takes.

Keep a clear vision in your head on why achieving your dream is so important to you and make sure you focus on that every single day. Then make it come true by following the steps I've outlined above. I believe in you. It's time you believe in you too!

Natalie Sisson is a Suitcase Entrepreneur who is on a mission to ensure others create freedom in business and adventure in life using online tools, social media and outsourcing to build a thriving online business you can take anywhere.

Creating your own Dream Design

Sometimes you wake up. Sometimes the fall kills you.
And sometimes, when you fall, you fly.
- Neil Gaiman

I'm not a former Chair of a Fortune 500 company.

I don't have a Master's degree in marketing.
I'm not a *"professional"* in any sense, as it relates to
the business world.

You know what?

It doesn't really bother me :)

Corporate America and I just don't mix. To be
honest with you, I like working. What I don't like, is
being treated like a machine, given a number, pushed
towards perfection, and in return--to be given a
paycheck that barely keeps my head above water.

Sure, I could have moved into a management
position and did at one time, against my greater
judgment. That led to packing up a couple bags and
moving to California to get out of the madness. It

almost killed my spirit. For what little pay raise I received, I was expected to work 50-60 hours a week.

That's insane!

I'm sorry, but doing a job that does nothing to fulfill me, is not worth that much time of my life, no matter how much money I'm making. Especially if it's for a company who is only driven by growth, profit, and power.

Maybe this made sense back in the days of the American Dream when you would work for one company for 30 years and be taken care of with a pension for the rest of your life, but those days are over. Most employees today are just numbers on a balance sheet and they are easily expendable. Working 50 or 60 hours a week for a company that will eliminate your position in an instant if it improves shareholder value just doesn't make sense to me.

I refuse to continue being beaten down by power, greed, and stupidity. I can't. It's got to stop. At the same time, I can't just quit. I have to provide for my family. So the beat goes on, da-da-dum da dum da-dah.

So that's why I'm creating my own Dream Design.

What does Dream Design mean Justin?

Glad you asked :). I dubbed the strategy I'm taking with me on my path to follow my dreams, **Dream Design**.

Dream design is the framework of your path to fulfillment. It is the structure for your journey to a better life. Dream Design is the road you walk on, while following your dreams. A Dream Design is your method to achieve those dreams. It is your strategy to change your life.

By learning how to perceive the world in a way, which opens up your inner ability to find your purpose, your message, and your story, you are able to share your gifts with the world. You begin to understand how to actually reach for those "Dreams" and use them to change your life, and ultimately change the world.

My Dream Design

My Dream Design process looks something like this:

o *Establish a Vision for the future*
o *Find my Purpose for Following my dreams*
o *Build Desire with Inspiration*
o *Build relationships with everyone I admire*

- *Plan to make it real, then act*
- *Work like I'm on vacation*
- *Take breaks, Have fun, Enjoy the ride*
- *Persevere through all Fear, Failures, & Setbacks*
- *Keep moving forward!!*
- *Change the world, change my life*

These are some of the things I do as part of my Dream design:

- *I push myself each and every day to be inspired, give inspiration, and take a step forward on my journey to change my life and the world.*
- *I do what I feel as I feel it*
- *I follow my passions for changing the world*
- *I follow my passions for entrepreneurship*
- *I read, write, and connect constantly*
- *I spend too much time checking email and social media channels*
- *I differentiate myself by being myself. I don't follow any specific plan; I mix them together and add my own flavor.*
- *I go with what feels right, not what I think will work*
- *I surround myself with the people who want what I want*

- *I work every single day and always keep pursuing the vision I have for the future of my life and that of the world, including everyone in it.*
- *I experiment, analyze, ask, and answer*
- *I am always trying to do something new*
- *I fight fear, negativity, and doubt with the people around me, and to shut them down when absolutely necessary.*
- *& more...*

How Can You Create Your Dream Design?
However you want!

There is nothing more liberating than knowing you have the capability within yourself to create the life you want to live. What's ultimately fulfilling is the journey you take to create that life, and the relationships you develop with people along the way.

Get your FREE **Dream Design** Toolkit at www.ChangeYourPerceptionBook.com

Follow Your Dreams: My Story of Fear, Failure, & Perseverance

Dreams are only an illusion, until you open your eyes and take actions to make them real.
- Justin Harmon

Back in the Day

There were many times in my life when I felt like a prisoner. A prisoner of the society I live in. A prisoner of my circumstances. A prisoner of my fears and doubts. A prisoner of expectations and responsibilities.

I felt like I didn't have a say in how I wanted my life to go. I always had big dreams growing up. As a kid, I wanted to be a professional baseball player. I had a vision of myself where I would be up to bat for my favorite team, (*St. Louis Cardinals*) and I would just be soaking up the moment as my family and friends looked on, along with a stadium full of cheering fans. You know what happened to that dream?

It died inside my mind. My biggest dream died because I was too shy to join the team when I was a kid. I'm not saying that I could have become a pro if I would have joined the team and kept playing, practicing, sacrificing, working hard, and believing the rest of the way. But *I may have.*

While I may not have become a pro baseball player, I could have overcome my shyness. I could have followed my little heart and just went for it. But I didn't. Years later, I finally joined a summer league for freshmen. My family and I had just moved to a new town, so naturally I didn't know anyone.

My four weeks with the team, led to no games started, five at bats, no hits, two walks, and one run scored. I wasn't very good. Then again, I had never played fast pitch before. The practices included the *"well known"* players that were already established getting all of the coaching. I was more of a benchwarmer and cheerleader than a baseball player.

Can you guess what I did? **I quit!**

Just like that, I quit. Because I wasn't getting any playing time or attention, I gave up. I gave up because I didn't think I was good enough. I quit because it was the easy thing to do. I could have let go of that self-doubt and shyness and worked my butt off to become the best that I could be. But I didn't.

That was as close as I got to my professional baseball career.

Why Should You Listen to Me?

I shared my story with you because everyone has a dream that (*they think*) is bigger than they are. I am sure you have had some kind of dream that seemed like it was out of reach. I did. I didn't think for a moment that my biggest dreams could ever be a reality. Not once. I would wish and dream and fantasize all the time, but nothing else. As I got older, I started to become more practical with the way I looked at my future goals and objectives. For a long time, I stopped dreaming.

Here's how that turned out. I have started and stopped college twice and I've had over 30 jobs. Yeah, looks like being practical worked out really well. My efforts simply led me to become unhappy with my life, party more, and care less. That bothered me. I knew that I wasn't someone who could be happy with doing the "*status quo*" thing, but I didn't believe I could do anything about it. I wouldn't have even known where to begin.

Learning and Experience

When I finally realized that I needed something more and that it would be physically impossible for me to be happy if I didn't love what I was doing, I started searching.

I searched high, low, and everywhere in between. I looked on the Internet and read books and blogs on online business and inspiration. I wasted money on get rich quick schemes. I didn't know what to do. I didn't have a purpose. I didn't have a clue. I spent over eight years experimenting, trying, and failing to find the golden ticket of my life. I wanted to essentially become rich enough to not have to work for corporate America. But I was asking the wrong questions!

I gave up again. I quit. I gave in to what everyone else around me was saying and decided I needed to get a good job and stay put. *"Plant some roots for your life. You need to settle down and face reality."* In my heart, I disagreed with the idea of doing things this way, but I did it because, *"that's just the way it is."* I moved back to my hometown, started working for a large distribution center in the area, fell in love with an amazing woman I ended up marrying, had a beautiful daughter, and started living the American Dream.

Alright. All of that's true except for the American Dream part. More like the road to hell! That's not to say I don't love and am not thankful for my family because I am. They are my world. But the old American Dream isn't my dream. To me it feels like diving off a cliff and forgetting that the water is six inches deep.

Follow Your Dreams

Suddenly, there I was. 27 years old, married, with a one-year-old child. I was the only one working because my wife wanted to stay home with our daughter while she was a baby. I wanted to be able to give them that opportunity and I had a good paying job for the area, so we were able to get by.

I had returned to college the year before and started to plan for the future. I still didn't know what I wanted to do. Because of the baby, school, work, and family life, I was home a lot. I was on the Internet a lot. I didn't want to admit it, but I was still looking for a replacement to this American Dream that was put upon me by society.

I was constantly searching for something new. I found something that intrigued me, only to look for something else a little while later.

I started reading **A LOT**. I was probably reading between two to three hours a night. That was all of the free time I had each day. I must have read about 20 books in six months. Not sure if that is considered a lot to you, but for me that was unheard of. I wasn't just reading to read either, I was reading to learn. I read every book I could find on inspiration, making a difference, online businesses and marketing, blogging, and overcoming fear and failure.

That led me to others who were living a new version of the American Dream. This version was based on helping others, making a difference in the world, and being passionate about what you do. There was an entire movement of people genuinely trying to make a difference in the world by living their passions and helping others. I was immediately in. I just didn't know where I would fit in. That is, until I took action.

That's not to say I started getting things right. I didn't! I started by getting them wrong but I was moving forward. I started and quit two blogs in a year. Those "mistakes" helped me find my own voice and figure out what I wanted to do. I couldn't just listen to other people, I had to figure this out for myself and taking action was what helped me figure it out.

Not long after, **Unplugged Recreated** was born. After everything I have learned, I was able to create and design a website, put the message I wanted to give to the world in words, help people, and have the opportunity to make a difference in the lives of others and in my own life.

You Gotta Keep Dreaming!

If you're like me, then you have no choice but to keep moving forward in pursuit of your life's dreams, because you cannot see it any other way. If you want to start dreaming again, begin to believe in yourself, your abilities, and your experiences. Use them as a tool for inspiration and motivation. Not only for yourself, but for others as well.

Dream big. Think Big. Take Big Actions! Follow Your Dreams

Follow your Dream without Quitting your Job

You want to follow your dream? You can't stand your job and you wish you had the ability to quit your job and focus on following your dreams.

The problem is, you may not have much savings. You may not even know how to follow your dreams, but you know you don't want to work for the man the rest of your life.

Whatever your situation, whether you want to quit your job to have more time to create your dream lifestyle design, or you want to quit your job because you can't stand it — it doesn't matter. As long as you want to want to quit your job and follow your dream, there are some things you should know.

You don't have to quit your job to follow your dream.

You don't need a lot of money to start following your dream.

You don't need a lot of time to start following your dream.

Some of the most common misconceptions about trying to build a lifestyle design for yourself are that you need to have a ton of time and money to follow your dreams. In the long run, yes. To achieve your dream life or lifestyle design you will have put in thousands of hours and make a few small investments.

Here's a quick tip: All you need to start is to take action. If it's an hour a day–reading, learning, and doing–that's 30 hours a month. If you use the time you do have efficiently, you can have quite a bit done in one month.

It's called baby steps. You know the saying, *"Rome wasn't built in a day;"* the same goes for dreams. Something of great magnitude takes time to complete.

If you look at a project that may potentially take six-to-eight months to complete, and you decide that the effort to accomplish it is not worth the reward of the project, you won't even start.

But, if you want to follow your dreams, knowing that the end result is a life that brings you freedom, fulfillment, and happiness, you should be willing to put in whatever amount of effort it takes.

What often derails so many people from putting in the extraordinary effort it takes to achieve their dreams is that they don't feel that the end result is possible.

Wrapping it up

What do we know? Here's a quick summary of why you don't have to quit your job to follow your dream.

It's a process. If you try to do everything at once, you will be overwhelmed, overworked, and under achieve. Following your dream takes time, effort, and passion. **Work with the time you have – even** if that's just an hour a day. If you focus on what needs to be done today, build a strategy for tomorrow, and keep taking action, you will already be further than 90% of everyone else.

Spend within your means. You don't have to pay thousands of dollars for experts to do the job for you. You can become the expert and learn everything yourself. Yes, it's more time, but haven't we established your dreams are worth it?

Just remember that the harder you make something, the harder it becomes. Mistakes will be made. You will fail, probably numerous times—but you will also learn, grow, and become better for it.

Don't quit your job until you feel confident and your dream starts to take flight – well, and until you have enough money to live off of!

Dreampreneurship
with Bruno Coelho

Entrepreneurship is experiencing a fundamental shift in this new Millennium.

Making money is no longer the driving force in our society. In fact, making money is impossible! The only thing you can do to have money, is to earn it.

And Dreampreneurs understand that. They know that achievement alone isn't enough because we're all wired for fulfillment – that is, we are willing to live and die for a worthwhile purpose that makes a meaningful impact beyond ourselves. In this new millennium you will witness the rise of **Dreampreneurship** – where Dreams, Entrepreneurs and Leadership meet to make a meaningful impact in the World.

We are Dreampreneurs!

We don't resonate with being a slave of someone else's dream. We need to feel that we're dedicating our lives to a worthwhile purpose. We are, first and foremost, leaders of ourselves. However, the next act of allowing others to join us on our journey toward greatness enriches the lives of everyone involved. We are dreamers who dream with our eyes wide open, thus turning our dreams into reality.

It's not that we're fearless. Rather, the fear of what our lives will look like if we don't follow our dreams is greater than **ALL** our other fears combined. For too long, we have divided the World between leaders and followers. Yet, we are all leaders. (Who's leading your Life?)!

Every extraordinary leader is a follower of something bigger and higher than themselves; a dream, a vision, a purpose. Every time we stop following greatness we start serving what's left--ourselves. Thus, the old hierarchy pyramid is being replaced by a network of leaders. This network is dynamically created every time a new quest calls us. We occupy dual roles; we are leaders and followers, teachers and students.

If you want to become a Dreampreneur, you need to start leading your Life beyond goals. It's not that goals aren't important, (they really are!) but they can be worthless WHEN:

*1) you don't know where you're going - **Leadership***

*2) you don't believe that you can do it - **Beliefs***
3) you don't see the journey ahead of you -
Visualization
*4) you don't have a plan to get you there - **Planning***
*5) you don't follow through - **Action***
*6) you don't have an auto-pilot to drive you - **Habits***

I have a question for you - are you a leader? No? Then who are you allowing to lead your life? That's one of the biggest myths about Leadership - the belief that to be a leader, one must hold a so called "*leadership position*." This false ideology is based on the premise that leadership signifies authority. Although authority and leadership have similarities, they are not one in the same. Leadership is influence. Right? Not exactly. Leadership does not equate influence if you're merely leading people to do something they *think* they want to do (when in reality they couldn't care less).

Leadership isn't nearly as much about your ability to influence others to follow you but about your ability to share your journey. So be a follower. A follower of your Heart. A follower of Hope. A follower of **Love!** Follow your inner being, and you will become a leader. Follow your heart and chase your dreams for your own fulfillment. Although we desire the support and recognition of friends, family, and coworkers, we don't NEED it. We do what we do because it is who we are. The moment we take up a cause bigger than ourselves, we are on the path to becoming an influential leader; and unstoppable force that will have a meaningful impact long after we are gone. Leadership isn't not about winning or success (*getting what you want*). It's about Glory – living your Values, serving your higher purpose and being willing to live and die for it!

You may have noticed my tendency to mix two opposite concepts: first with follower and leader, and now with life versus death. Why do I consider them to not be truly antagonistic concepts? Because they aren't competing against each other. They are complementing each other. Glory simply means that you're willing to LIVE (with every breath you take) and DIE to serve a higher purpose. When you make that decision... it doesn't matter how bad the storm looks or how big the army is... because you've become unstoppable. The purpose of Life isn't to survive as long as we can. The purpose of Life is to live as meaningful as we can. If you make this decision in your Heart, you'll be LIGHT YEARS ahead of everyone else because everyone else is afraid. Afraid of failing. Afraid of what might happen IF something happens. But you're more afraid of making your Life worthless by not following through on what you believe, deep down in your soul, is yours – GLORY.

Now it's time to talk about your Beliefs and how they influence the amount and type of actions you take AND the results you get in the process. But first I'm curious about something - have you ever heard of flea training? Flea training was popular in 1981, and involved merely a glass jar and a lid. In this process, the fleas are placed inside the jar and the lid is sealed. They are left undisturbed for three days. When the jar is opened, the fleas will not jump out. In fact, the fleas will never jump higher than the level set by the lid. Their behavior will now be set for the rest of their lives. In fact, these fleas will produce offspring who will automatically follow their example.

This issue goes beyond the scope of a few organizations with some self-serving leaders. What I am addressing here is how our current economic revolution is deeming our education system obsolete and training people to FAIL!

Today, there are no rules for you to follow in order to be successful. Today, the answers that you were told are obsolete. Today, if you want to fit in you'll become invisible and irrelevant!

The BIG question is - how HIGH will you jump?

The answer depends on what you believe you are capable of. The interesting thing about flea training is that the fleas didn't lose their ability to jump high. Rather, they lost the belief that they could exceed the limits to which they had been conditioned. Our Beliefs influence the amount and type of action we create from ALL of our potential. Thus, our actions, which are based on realizing our own potential, directly influence our results. The results will, in turn, either reinforce the Belief (I can do this) or make it weaker (I can't do this).

Visualization

Ayelet Fishbach and Jinhee Choi found out in 2012 that "describing the goals of working out boosted the students' intentions to exercise". Now get this - "the students who focused on their goals actually ended up running on the treadmill for less time than the students focused on the experience" (34 minutes versus 43 minutes) Visualizing the journey and seeing what obstacles you might face along the way is a great way to raise your chances of being successful! However, this can start to work against you if you get addicted to visualizing just by itself. What you're really doing is tricking your brain into believing that you've already arrived!

The question then becomes, how much is enough? Visualize how things will look like once you get there and see how you're able to overcome the obstacles that are in your way. But please... just get going! No amount of visualization can replace the actual work that you need to do to make it happen! And no amount of visualization can help you predict what's going to come (much less how it's going to unfold). You have to *see* what you want in your mind first, so you can recognize an opportunity later!

Planning

Don't mistake a plan for planning. The moment you have a static plan is the moment it becomes useless. Every New Year people make plans. And that's great! They think about what they want for their lives and (some) create a plan to make it happen. Then what happens? Six months later they couldn't care less about what they wanted to achieve in the first place. Why? Because unlike a plan, we change! That's what makes us Human and that's what makes us remarkable! Even Nature is constantly changing in small mutations and evolving over time. Why should *WE* be any different? The problem is that we attach our sense of self-worth and significance to our goals. Instead of using goals as a way to track progress on our journey, we use them as a way to measure our self-worth. That's why we hold on to our goals even when we don't care about them anymore. What would others think about us? We want to be seen as someone who finishes what we start, don't we? After all consistency builds trust!

If the only thing that keeps you going is that you're afraid of what others might think of you... you've already failed. What's your "plan?" Is it to just keep going, investing your time and energy into something that you don't believe in anymore? What does that say about you? What kind of standards do you have for yourself? That's the only thing that matters. Gollwitzer Research did some very interesting research on Symbolic Self-Completion. He discovered that "those who kept their intentions private were more likely to achieve their goals." If I had to suggest a reason why I would say that it's because they're not afraid of what might happen if they fail and they are also motivated to show the World what they've been working on! How long can you hold a secret? Then hurry up and finish that project!

This is your life. As the leader of your life you get to decide the values that are going to guide your journey! You get to set the goals you're using to measure your progress and when they don't serve you anymore... remove them! Lying is terrible, but the worst possible person you can lie to is yourself! So let's be honest here-- what's the reason you want to forget about that goal? I mean, the REAL reason. See we have to be really careful here because this strategy doesn't work if we lie to ourselves. If the reason why is based in fear, you have to keep going! Why?! Because that's a sign that you're challenging things and that's the moment when things change - when you decide that you're not settling for anything less! Bottom line is that goals don't measure your self-worth. Goals measure your progress. Plans are useless if they are static because Life isn't static. You should be able to seize every opportunity that you create instead of being worried about pursuing goals that don't serve you anymore.

Action

All that you've read right now. This entire book. All of the messages within are useless, if you don't take action. You can think about what kind of Life you want to lead. You can think about how you're going to master your fears and create empowering beliefs. You can visualize your journey all day long. You can have a brilliant plan. However, if you don't take action it's ALL worthless. Now here's something that you don't come across often enough: hard-work doesn't guarantee your success. But not working at all will guarantee your failure. However, hard-work is completely over-rated. It's being taught that hard-work and persistence are the magic formula for being successful. This formula is missing some important points that you should be aware of.

1. You can work-hard and be persistent in your efforts and still not be successful.
It might just not happen for you. When you read the examples of successful people it's easy to fall into the narrative fallacy that explains why it happened. But

the reality is really much more complex and unpredictable than it appears when you look at the past. So instead of trying to "motivate" yourself into a state of total certainty and confidence that you're going to be successful (because your brain at some point along the way will go: "who are you kidding?"), I would suggest you answer this question: "What is worth my hard-work and persistence EVEN if it doesn't turn out the way I expected it to be?"

2. *Being persistent doesn't mean being stubborn.* That's why some people use motivation the wrong way. If I see you banging your head against the wall when there's a door next to it, why should I tell you that you need more motivation to keep going?   "I can do it. I CAN do it! I CAN DO IT" affirmations won't do you any good if you're not taking action in a strategic way! There's always a way but it doesn't have to be the way that you're using right now! Focus on what you want to achieve but be flexible, ("like water" as Bruce Lee would say) on the how! However, also have this in your mind: absence of evidence doesn't mean evidence of absence. What this means is that just because you're not seeing any results, it doesn't mean that you're not making an

impact. You're just not measuring the right variable or perhaps the impact that you're making is impossible to measure. For instance, I'm a huge fan of Goa Gil (if you don't know him don't worry). But how can he know? Apart from some views on some YouTube videos and a like on his page, he couldn't know how much I care about him and the impact of what he's doing. In fact, I've never bought a CD from him. Unfortunately, I didn't have the chance to see him live, (I'm crossing my fingers for next year) but even so, he has been a HUGE influence on my podcast that mixes trance music with personal development! Be careful with how you are using the information you're getting from what you're measuring.

Habits

And finally, we've come up to what I like to call our auto-pilot. Habits. Parking the car and then wondering 10 minutes later if you locked it - did this ever happen to you? Or having no electricity in your house (during a blackout) but you still tried to turn the lights on when you were looking for the flash light, didn't you? Why? Because much of our behavior is driven by our unconscious mind. In fact, scientists led by Professor John-Dylan Haynes from the Max Planck Institute for

Human Cognitive and Brain Sciences "used a brain scanner to investigate what happens in the human brain just before a decision is made". What they found out is that "it was possible to predict from brain signals which option participants would take already seven seconds before they consciously made their decision!" Yes. It's that powerful.

The good news is that good habits are just as addictive as bad habits (and are much more rewarding)! So how can you develop empowering habits? Researchers say that you need three things: a trigger (something that ignites the action); the ritual (the action itself) and the reward (that is used to reinforce the habit). How long does it take to form a habit? Researchers Benjamin Gardner and Susanne Meisel concluded that "for one person it took just 18 days, and another did not get there in the 84 days, but was forecast to do so after as long as 254 days. The best estimate is 66 days, but it's unwise to attempt to assign a number to this process."

In other words - it takes as long as it needs to take. But here's something that Dr. Russell Poldrack, a neurobiologist at the University of Texas at Austin, found that you can use to create your habits faster than anyone else - "enjoyable behaviors can prompt your brain to release a chemical called dopamine. If you do something over and over, and dopamine is there when you're doing it, it strengthens the habit even more. When you're not doing those things, dopamine creates the craving to do it again." This is why your "going to the gym habit" doesn't last. Your brain doesn't like stress! And who can blame it, right? This will keep happening until you make sure that you're having pleasure in whatever the activity you want to create as a habit! If you find a way to make your time in the gym pleasurable, your brain won't go "Hell no! I'm not going into that place again" anymore! Perhaps, if you look for ways to become healthier and have fun in the process, your brain might go, "well... I like going to the beach... Why not play volleyball for an hour giving all we've got in the process?"

Now it's up to you. I hope that you'll take what you've read and use it to create your own meaningful Dreampreneurship journey!

Bruno Coelho is a Portuguese Dreampreneur that created TheRabbitWay.com to equip and empower other Dreampreneurs with the software and people development skills they need to start living a Life worth dying for.

The Entrepreneurial Leap
with John Lee Dumas

It sounds so daunting; but it doesn't have to be.

After interviewing over 200 successful Entrepreneurs, I have seen many traits shared in commonality. However, there is only one trait that every single Entrepreneur has in common.

They started. Every single Entrepreneur who has amassed wealth, fame, or success on any level has done so because at some point in their path they took that first, tentative, awkward baby step forward.

For me, it was attending a conference called Blog world in NYC. I knew what I wanted EntrepreneurOnFire to become, but I had no clue how to connect with the successful Entrepreneurs who would make my dream a reality. Blog world was the lion's den, and I walked into it unarmed, but ready to do battle.

I left that conference with many great memories, but most importantly, many confirmed guests of Entrepreneurs who would make up the backbone of EntrepreneurOnFire.

EntrepreneurOnFire is a podcast that shares the journey of our spotlighted guest. We talk about facing and overcoming our failures. We talk about AHA moments and turning those AHA moments into success. We talk about what excites people and their vision for the future.

We end every interview with a five question lightning round. The first question in this lightning round sets the tone for the following four.

"What was holding you back from becoming an Entrepreneur?"

Fear. 99% of my guests reply with some variance of that word if not that word itself. 1% respond "*nothing was holding me back*." This is Entrepreneur talk for "I was scared out of my mind."

If I could add one more question to this lightning round it would be, "What is the thing you are most grateful for in regards to your Entrepreneurial journey?"

I know with full confidence what 99% of the answers would be.

"That I started. That I stopped the excuses, swallowed my fear, my pride, the imaginary obstacles, and I started."

What are your excuses?

When are you going to "**Just start**"?

John Lee Dumas is the Founder and Host of EntrepreneurOnFire, a business podcast that interviews today's most inspiring and successful Entrepreneurs seven days a week. EntrepreneurOnFire is a top ranked business podcast generating over 175,000 unique downloads a month in over 145 countries with a lineup of Barbara Corcoran, Seth Godin, Tim Ferriss, Gary Vaynerchuk, Guy Kawasaki, and hundreds more.

25 Excuses to Wait on Your Dreams
with Lori Deschene

"The best day of your life is the one on which you decide your life is your own. No apologies or excuses...The gift is yours—it is an amazing journey—and you alone are responsible for the quality of it."
- Bob Moawad

If we try, we can always find a reason *not* to do what we want to do—and it can seem perfectly valid. We can convince ourselves that we're being smart, realistic, or safe, or that we don't even really want it.

We're great at justifying the status quo, because we know exactly what that's like—even if it's dissatisfying.

The unknown can feel terrifying. But somewhere in that same realm where anything can go wrong is everything that can go right.

So many times in my life, I've finally pushed myself to do something and then wondered, "Why did I wait so long?" If I had known the benefits would far outweigh my fear and discomfort, I would have pushed myself sooner.

But we can't ever know that in advance. We can only know that our reasons to do something are greater than our excuses not to.

In my efforts to keep moving beyond my comfort zone, I've compiled the top 25 excuses not to go after a dream, along with a few reminders to help us overcome them.

Excuses About Time
1. I'm too busy to do what I love.
2. I don't have time to discover what I'm passionate about.
3. I've already put a lot of time into a different path.
4. I'll do it—*someday*.
5. It's too late for me now.

We all have the same number of hours in each day, and we all have the potential to use them to do what we want to do.

That being said, we're all starting with different schedules, responsibilities, and obstacles. A single, childless person who inherited a large sum of money may have more immediate time and freedom than someone with a large family and mounting debt.

I share this not to be discouraging, but rather to acknowledge reality: We all have unique circumstances that could make it challenging to find or make time.

While it might be easier for some of us,
it's possible for all of us.

We can all create at least a small window of time to take one simple step. We can all decide our dreams are priorities, and that we owe it to ourselves to pursue them, regardless of what we've done previously. We can all recognize that it's never too late for us unless we decide it is.

The important thing to realize is that the time is now, whether we have days, hours, or even just minutes to devote. We might not have the time to do everything, but we all have the time to do something.

Excuses About Money
6. I don't have the money to get started.
7. I need to continue earning exactly what I earn now.

8. I can't make any changes until I pay off my debt.

9. I need a bigger safety net before I take a risk.

10. What if I can't make any money at it?

We all need money to live—there's just no getting around it.

We may sometimes have to do things we don't love to get by, and we may not all be able to completely change our lives overnight. We might not be able to up and travel the world, or make massive financial investments in our goals.

What we *can* do is decide that our dreams are important, and then leverage our most valuable resource—our passion—to honor them as best we can.

That might mean doing something on the side as a hobby, or bartering for free lessons, or volunteering our time to help someone who will serve as a mentor.

We don't need a massive amount of money to start, or a guarantee that we'll make a ton of money down the line.

We just need to know that our dreams are worth the effort, and that we're willing to be creative with the resources we have.

Excuses About Knowledge

11. I don't know where to start.

12. I don't know enough to start.

13. I'm not smart enough to succeed.

14. I don't know if I can make it.

15. I'm not an expert.

No one knows going in exactly what they need to do—or what they *can* do. No one has it all figured out, and no one starts off with expertise.

If we wait until we feel we know everything we need to know, we'll likely never act.

When I wrote for a 'tween publication, I interviewed a young girl named Leah Larson who started a magazine called Yaldah at 13 years old.

She wrote all the articles for the first issue herself, and then made countless calls to printers and potential advertisers, having no idea what she was doing. Perhaps because she was so young, she never worried about what she didn't know. She just jumped in and started learning.

Ten years later, Yaldah has expanded to Yaldah Media Inc., which now offers books, retreats, and more. She's grown with her company, as we all can with any dream.

We don't need to know everything to start. We just need to know we want and then do it.

Excuses About Other People

16. My friends and family don't think I can do this.
17. My friends and family don't think I *should* do this.
18. I need to focus on the people who need me.
19. I don't have anyone to do this with.
20. It's all about who you know—and I don't know the right people.

There will never be a day when everyone agrees with us, believes in us, and supports us. There may never be a time when other people stop needing us. And for many of us, there won't be a likeminded partner waiting to hold our hand on a parallel journey.

If we believe in ourselves, none of these things have to deter us. As we do what we love and create new possibilities for ourselves, we will inevitably form mutually beneficial relationships. In my early days on Twitter, I had a different account where I tweeted uplifting messages. It was my first attempt at making the difference I wanted to make.

Back then, I'd never have imagined I'd be connected to so many amazing people; and I wasn't sure I could run a website since I knew nothing about the tech side of things.

One day, a web strategist and designer named Joshua Denney tweeted about me, complimenting my profile and tweets. Since our initial connection, he's been instrumental in shaping Tiny Buddha—and he's become one of my closest confidantes, consultants, and friends.

There are countless people out there who could support and help us, but we can only meet them if we put ourselves out there.

Excuses About Probability

21. Things likely wouldn't pan out.

22. Many people have tried to do this and failed.

23. I'll probably be scared and uncomfortable if I try.

24. I'm not sure if this is the "right" decision.

25. There aren't any guarantees.

The reality is there *aren't* any guarantees. That means even a sure thing could one day be uncertain. Certainty is an illusion that comes from comfort—but just because something's comfortable doesn't mean it's permanent.

We can either cling to what feels safe, avoiding potential disappointment, or realize the worst disappointment is the type we feel in ourselves.

That's what happens when we ignore our calling; we may feel more secure for not taking a risk, but we also feel unhappy with ourselves for not finding the courage to do it.

We can't ever know what the results of our efforts will be, but we can know that we dramatically increase our odds of feeling satisfied if we make it a priority to do what we love—no matter where it leads us.

That's what it means to make the "right" decision—to do what feels right, right in this moment, the only moment that's guaranteed.

And one more excuse I didn't include

I'm not good enough. We've all thought this at one time or another. In our socially connected world where we have constant reminders of everyone else's achievements, it's easy to feel we don't stack up.

But maybe we don't have to. Maybe we don't need to be better than anyone else, or even better than we are now in order to make a difference.

Maybe the world needs us exactly as we are, with our unique blend of skills, talent, and potential. Maybe the difference we make isn't just about where we end up, but also about how we learn, grow, and share on the way there.

Sure, our gifts and accomplishments can make the world a better place, but what we really want and need is to be inspired—and what's more inspiring than starting right where you are, believing in yourself, and taking a leap of faith?

When we're feeling overwhelmed, it can seem like dreams are luxuries, but they're not reserved for the chosen few. They're reserved for people who choose to believe in them and take action.

To do that, we need to stop telling ourselves the story of why we can't, and start creating the story of how we can.

What's your dream and what can you do today to start living it?

*Lori Deschene is the founder of Tiny Buddha, a
community blog that features stories and insights
from readers from all over the globe. Since it
launched in 2009, Tiny Buddha has grown into one of
the most popular inspirational sites on the web, with
more than 1.5 million monthly readers. Lori is the
author of* Tiny Buddha's Guide to Loving Yourself
*and the Tiny Wisdom eBooks series, and co-founder
of the online course Recreate Your Life Story: Change
the Script and Be the Hero.*

Section Six:
Moving Forward

First Steps Insights

"I'm a big fan of doing research before starting an ambitious project. Knowledge is a weapon against fear and doubt, because you can begin to see how the success would be realized. Talking to other people who ran businesses helped me wrap my head around the challenges and figure out a path to starting my own."
- Scott H Young

"The important thing to keep in mind -- and this sounds obvious, but still almost nobody heeds it -- is that your decisions are always up to you. All rules (and even laws) are simply someone else's opinion. The idea of a thing being "normal" just means that currently, more people hold that opinion than hold a differing opinion.

The next time you think you "have to" do something -- be it going to work, owning a phone, buying gifts at Christmastime, or even paying your rent -- stop and recognize the truth: You do not HAVE to do those things in any literal sense. If you don't pay your rent, you'll get evicted... but you CAN not pay it.

The same is true for almost anything we think is an absolute.

The minute you start realizing that everything you face and everything you ultimately do is your choice, and you start to make truly conscious decisions, the sooner your life is truly in your hands."
- Johnny B Truant

A New Definition of Success
with Debashish Das

Society's definition treats success like a unit of measure. Just like miles or kilometers run indicate if you have completed a 10k or a marathon, success is supposed to indicate how well you have done in life.

But, success is not something that can be counted, so how do you measure how well you are doing?

By measuring and comparing tangible parameters - most common of which is money. It is a universal concept. More wealth equals more success, couldn't be simpler. And as you know, the more successful you are, happier you will be.

Is that really the case though?

Why do studies indicate that beyond a certain amount of wealth, money has no role to play in peoples' happiness?

Almost everybody I've met believes money to be the best motivation to do anything. However, amassing wealth for its own sake is like gathering sticks in the forest without the intention of starting a fire. Money is a means to an end. The real question is;

what are you going to do the day after you achieve the amount of wealth you set out to? If you can die happy on the next day, you can stop reading right here.

Mostly though, I expect the answers to be - own a beach house, buy a Ferrari, and visit Thailand etc. If so, it isn't truly the money you are after. It is the experience that money will buy.

You can apply this technique to any answer on your journey towards creating a life of your own creation. Then, you will reach an important crossroad. To go out and achieve this end as soon as possible, or to spend the rest of your life amassing wealth, always waiting to start your journey towards this end.

If you have stuck with me so far, I'll give you a shortcut. The answer you are looking for is "happiness". This in itself is not an objective to achieve, but rather a state to be in. Only you know what will make you happy.

How much soul searching or self-examination you do to get this answer is up to you. Put enough effort into it and you will realize that, the end result of attaining any kind of success will always be happiness.

You slog away at your desk, eight hours daily, or put in a twelve hour business day because of an imagined *happy retirement*.

Your reasons might be as varied as putting the family needs first; to be the best in the industry; to become rich, or to go on a world tour.

The motivation to endure hardship does not come from the objective itself. It is the experience or feeling that you will get after accomplishing that objective. Just thinking about one million dollars in your bank account or a world cruise with your family makes your day better.

The imagination of achievement of this end is a powerful motivator, holding you on the path of hard work, making you endure daily misery. Or, as society often puts it, 'striving for success'. Everybody and their uncle have put success on a pedestal and have set about worshipping it. When you are born, you are blissfully unaware of the world and enjoy living life.

As you grow up, you see everybody making a beeline for this thing called "success". You can see it from afar, shining like a beacon.

But you don't quite understand what it is, so the people around you show you visions - money, big houses, luxurious cars, and importance in the eyes of men. It is what all of them want, and as a result, it becomes something you want.

A phenomenon aptly described by the definition of Ubuntu (as popularized by Nelson Mandela), "I am who I am because of who we all are." Society's definition of success becomes your definition of success.

Have you ever thought about the pedestal that forms the base for success?

The secret of success is not in striving for it, but in building a solid foundation. The stronger and higher the pedestal, the clearer success appears. If you have such a base, whatever you put on that pedestal shines like a beacon, and is seen as success. Happiness is that base. Society's definition puts result before reason. Success doesn't cause happiness, it results from it.

It took some time and effort, but I have been able to discover quite a bit about what makes me happy. Based on my discovery, I have created my own definition of living a successful life. I share it in the hope that something might resonate with you, or at least cause you to think about what really makes you happy.

1. Be the master of my own time

I value my freedom above all else. Deciding what I do with the limited time I have is an expression of that freedom. What's the point of the fat paycheck if I don't have the freedom to spend money the way I like? I'd much rather go on a road trip on my bike than spend the week at my desk, getting paid for ass in the chair time.

2. Enjoy Life

Life is meant to be enjoyed. I don't just want to write a bucket list, I want to live it. Bungee jumping is one thing I enjoy, and I want to do the highest one there is (New Zealand, 550m high). I would prefer to do it next year rather than wait till I am 60, when I might be physically unable to do it.

3. Do the work that I love

As Scott Dinsmore says, "*If you don't do something for your own reasons, you'll either do it terribly, be terribly unhappy doing it, or both.*"

I acknowledge that money (the reason I work) is necessary for survival, but it is a fixed amount and varies from person to person. I'd be happy at half of my current salary, if it came from doing something that I love, enjoy, and do every day (like writing).

4. Build and maintain genuine relationships

Friends and family are my emotional support base. I know they want to share in my life and happiness because they care for me and their happiness means the world to me.

I cannot share happiness with them unless I am happy first. I can share in their sorrow only when I have no sorrow of my own. I have decided to make relationships a priority in life; to build and maintain them based on happiness.

5. Help others

Helping other people is the best source of happiness. It can be in the form of tutoring the kid next door, volunteering at a retirement home, helping a friend do his homework, or carrying a neighbor's groceries to their home.

If done selflessly with no expectation of return, the resulting happiness is immeasurable. I want to help others find happiness, just as I have found mine. It is the way I choose to give of myself.

6. Fitness

I believe society's definition of success falls flat on its face when pitted against fitness (physical, mental, spiritual and social).

If I am not fit, I won't be able to enjoy life, my free time will spent in hospitals or therapy, the money I get from work will be spent on medicines, family members and friends will always be worried, and I definitely won't be of help to anyone. I have decided to make fitness a priority.

I derive happiness from it because it enables me to live life to the fullest.

I have defined my success as living life happily. I know what makes me happy, and hard work is a price I will gladly pay for it.

Success is not a 'one size fits all' concept. It is as individual as you are. Find out what success really means to you. As Leo Babauta (of Zenhabits) puts it, ***"If success can be anything, then it is nothing."***

Debashish Das is the author of the blog quitbefree.com, where he writes about the lessons learned on his journey of self-discovery.

Common Mistakes
with Stephanie Waasdorp

There were three common mistakes I made starting out on the road of entrepreneurship.

Armed with my Social Studies degree, a whole lot of quirky ideas and self-confidence, I started my business in 2009. That meant that I subscribed at the chamber of commerce. Despite my confidence and enthusiasm, I made a lot of mistakes. And I still do, by the way. Here are three of them.

#1 Having a chamber of commerce number and thinking you're in business already.

Even though it felt great to see my entrepreneurial status on paper, this meant nothing, because there was no business yet. In my mind, in my dreams, yes, there was a business. I could see myself on stage, managing all these projects and people, having a huge following and operating as one of the most inspirational young female leaders of the future. (Yes, I dream BIG!) But the reality was that I had none of that. Yes, there was now this green light flashing in front of me: 'Miss

Waasdorp is now officially a business owner. She can start!' But… next question was: where to start? That leads me to the next mistake:

#2 Thinking that great ideas and great people will come to you

No! They won't. Nobody knows you and nobody is interested in your ideas. Not until you've convinced them that your ideas are valuable, profitable, unique, awesome, new, inspirational, possible, etc.

And that alone is one hell of a job. Because once you start brainstorming about your ideas, you will discover that nearly everything is already being done by somebody else. And *that* somebody else is much more advanced than you-- that person has a following already and people know their name and their business. Then there's you; a nobody. I still feel like "a nobody" from time to time. Because the fact is, I am. At least, if I compare myself to the experts in my field who are already "a somebody." And if I do that, it makes me feel like I'm not enough. This leads me to mistake number three.

#3 Thinking your own ideas, knowledge and creativity are not enough

I've talked to a lot of business owners in the last couple of years and I think this is a common thought we all have on occasion. To speak for myself, I've been pretty overwhelmed by all the possibilities and competition. What was important for me was to do things anyway, despite my doubts and fears. I still have a big dream for myself, my life and for the world. I want to ignite change; to do something to improve the world. I have to do something about the issues we face in today's world. I have to use my creative entrepreneurial mind. The world needs it because I know I can add value. The world needs me. And the world needs you as well. As I'm continuing on the path of entrepreneurship, I start to realize more and more that I am enough, that my ideas are worthy, and that my knowledge is sufficient to make a difference. The difference I am making is small right now. But for the few people I've helped, it's big. Their lives have been changed for the better.

And that's how I change the world: one person at a time. One step at a time. One blog post at a time. One idea at a time. One thought at a time. If I can do it, you can do it. Just never ever give up on your dreams, do whatever it takes, and meanwhile: enjoy this wild, crazy and bumpy ride!

Stephanie Waasdorp helps introverts to be confident with who they are, through coaching and training. She also writes a lot about love, her favorite subject. 'Love who you are, and everything else will become much more easy', is her life motto. twitter.com/StephanieWaa

Freedom to Move Forward

Sometimes I wake up and forget where I am. For a moment I can sense a piece of my past from years ago. I think about my future and where I want to be. Where I want to go from today. How I'm going to get there. I lose myself in thought and end up somewhere I know I could never be.

The Depths of an Eccentric Mentality

My mind is a canyon of scattered thoughts and broken dreams. With each new day comes a new path I want to take. I'm focused on my intentions in my current choices, yet believe I can always do more. Be better.

I imagine myself as the person I want to be and neglect the person I am. The person I've become. My inner world is a fantasy land of hopes, desires, and dreams that plague me with their depths of nothingness. I'm a walking talking zombie with no real motivation to put my thoughts into action. I get stuck often and leave my mind for days at a time just to escape the infinite direction it leads me.

Progress is a Seesaw

After being away, the urge starts to build. There is a spark within me that won't allow me to rest. It's a point in my heart that wants to expand. So, I start to move forward. I start to progress once more into the abyss of myriad ideation. I wander through the chambers of my heart in search of the next act.

What I often find, is an ever growing knowing of the reasons for my regression. It's the moments of stonewall that fuel the ability to grow, to move forward. I find that in the times of low ambitions, my ability to truly take a step forward is increased ten-fold. The hardest part is the first step. Once my route begins to take shape, my speed increases, and my destination becomes clear.

It's not so much about the end of the journey, rather the progress that's made towards fulfillment in the cycle.

Finding Freedom in the Story

"The heart wants what it wants – or else it does not care"
- Emily Dickenson

I find that quote to be fairly accurate. If my heart is into what I'm seeking, it lifts me up to another level and pushes me forward in leaps and bounds. If my heart's just not into what I'm seeking, it will simply just not show up. When my heart's not into it, whatever IT is, everything just becomes mundane. Perhaps that's where the true freedom to move forward lies.

Your heart will not always be on. It's there when you need it, but can also remain silent to allow you to choose. To choose to take the next step. To do the work that's somewhat unfavorable. It's like sending a child off on a bike on their own for the first time. You're the heart, the inspiration, the guide. You can only hold on so long, but it's up to your child to start peddling. It's up to them to use the guidance to build momentum and then ride on.

The freedom in your story is in the moments when the heart silences and the ability to push your story forward is challenged. If you live up to the challenge, your heart will follow. If you can find the strength to push through the noise. To push through the challenges. The parts of your story that you don't really care to do. If you can stay the course, even when it becomes tedious and boring, you'll soon see just how free you truly are to choose for yourself.

Some say follow your heart. I say let your heart guide you and then let something deeper move you forward. Overcome what your mind tells you and trust your heart to lead you, even when your heart doesn't seem to care. Trust in the freedom of your own story. You may not end up where you wanted to go, but you will end up where you were meant to be.

Acknowledgements

Edited by: Sarah Vedolich

Special Guest Writers

Amy Clover - StrongInsideOut.com

John Lee Dumas - EntrepreneurOnFire.com

A.J. Leon - Misfit-Inc.com

Srinivas Rao - BlogcastFM.com

Natalie Sisson - SuitcaseEntrepreneur.com

Lori Deschene - TinyBuddha.com

Liz Seda - ALifeOnYourTerms.com

JD Roth - JDRoth.com

Pace Smith - PaceAndKyeli.com

Scott Dinsmore - LiveYourLegend.net

Johnny B. Truant - JohnnyBTruant.com

Scott H. Young - ScottHYoung.com

Sibyl Chavis - PossibilityOfToday.com

Jennifer Gresham - EverydayBright.com

Debashish Das - quitbefree.com

Alden Tan - Alden-Tan.com

Karen Renee - Kareneeart.com

Bruno Coelho - TheRabbitWay.com

Stephanie Waasdorp - StephanieWaasdorp.com

Jesicka Labud - TwoNonTechies.com

Charles Eisenstein - Sacred Economics Author & Speaker

A Special Thanks

This book would not have been possible if it weren't for those who supported me. The community of people who inspired and empowered me to keep moving forward and persist above all efforts. To Meaghan and Roxy for being my lights through the darkness and biggest fans; I love you and couldn't have done it without both of your support. I want to thank my Dad for always supporting my endeavors I appreciate everything you've done for me. My Mom for encouraging me to dream and always being there.

Jonathan Mead for giving me a community to grow and learn from. You've been a great inspiration to me and have fully supported me on my path.

Sarah Vedolich for being the Rock star you are. Thank you so much for being there right when I needed you.

I want to personally thank all the backers to the Indiegogo campaign that believed in this book and the messages shared within.

Thank you Cathy Potter, Thomas Morkes, A.J. Leon, John Lee Dumas, Randy Chongolio Bain, Debashish Das, Bruno Coelho, Natalie Sisson, and everyone who has encouraged and supported me along the way.